INTERRELIGIOUS DOCUMENTS I

Guidelines for Dialogue between Christians and Muslims

◇◇◇◇◇◇◇◇

Pontifical Council for Interreligious Dialogue

◇◇◇◇◇◇◇◇

Prepared by Maurice Borrmans
Translated from the French by R. Marston Speight

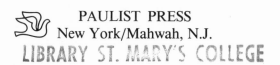

PAULIST PRESS
New York/Mahwah, N.J.

Library of Congress Cataloging-in-Publication Data

Borrmans, Maurice.
    [Orientations pour un dialogue entre chrétiens et musulmans. English]
    Guidelines for dialogue between Christians and Muslims/by Pontifical Council for Interreligious Dialogue: a new edition prepared by Maurice Borrmans; translated from the French by R. Marston Speight.
        p.   cm.
    Translation of: Orientations pour un dialogue entre chrétiens et musulmans. 1981.
    Includes bibliographical references and index.
    ISBN 0-8091-3181-1 (paper)
    1. Islam—Relations—Christianity.   2. Christianity and other religions—Islam.   I. Catholic Church. Pontifical Council for Interreligious Dialogue.   II. Title.
    BP172.B6713   1990
    261.2'7—dc20   90-41132
                                                                            CIP

Published by Paulist Press
997 Macarthur Boulevard
Mahwah, New Jersey 07430

Printed and bound in the
United States of America

Contents

Foreword

The impetus to interreligious dialogue given by the Second Vatican Council found a concrete expression in a series of booklets published by the Secretariat for Non-Christians around 1970. These aimed at providing theoretical and practical indications regarding the encounter with the followers of the major religious traditions of the world. Among these publications was a slim volume entitled *Guidelines for Dialogue between Christians and Muslims*. Translated into various languages, it was soon out of print. It can be said to have played an historic, and in some ways a pioneering, role. Ten years later it was decided to bring out a new edition, taking into account the experience of Christian-Muslim relations in the intervening period. The task of preparing this new edition was entrusted to Fr. Maurice Borrmans who combines a deep knowledge of the sources and the development of Islam with much practical experience in dialogue with Muslims.

The result is no ordinary book. It is the fruit of wide knowledge and practical experience, but above all of much reflection in order to find the "right word" with which to speak about our Muslim brothers and sisters. And the right word is that which is inspired by love, as the Christian writer Ferdinand Ebner has pointed out. This book, born out of love, aims at promoting that "civilization of love" which will be possible only when partners recognize the image given of them to be a faithful one. Knowledge of one another and mutual relations are true and sincere in proportion to the love that one bears for the other. Love is the only way to overcome the gap which will always exist between one's knowledge of the other (interpretation by another) and that person's self-knowledge (self-interpretation). Dialogue and communication can really take place only when self-interpretation and interpretation by another coincide in love.

This is of particular importance for Christian-Muslim relations. The images we carry of one another do not correspond to our own self-understanding. As W. Montgomery Watt has remarked:

> Among the world's major religions it is certainly Islam that the Westerner has the most difficulty in approaching objectively. The reasons for this are rooted in past history. Because of the Crusades, in the 12th and 13th Centuries many learned people in the West wanted the

1

religion of Islam to be better known. But the image they portrayed of Islam can be quite accurately qualified as 'distorted.' Western opinion about Islam and Muslims was based for centuries on this 'distorted image.' Even the more objective research of the last hundred and fifty years has not entirely succeeded in correcting the image of Islam in the minds of present-day Western observers.

It was because of the persistence of this distorted issue that the Second Vatican Council declared:

> Although in the course of the centuries many quarrels and hostilities have arisen between Christians and Muslims, this most sacred Synod urges all to forget the past and to strive sincerely for mutual understanding. On behalf of all mankind, let them make common cause of safeguarding and fostering social justice, moral values, peace, and freedom (*Nostra Aetate,* No. 3).

Christian-Muslim encounter finds its deepest motivation, and its platform, in faith in the One God, Almighty and Merciful, Creator of the world and Lord of history, who will judge and requite human beings according to their deeds. Vatican II was clear on this point, and since then the Popes have constantly emphasized the spiritual bond between Muslims and the followers of Jesus Christ. "I believe," said Pope John Paul II on the memorable occasion of his meeting with young Muslims in Casablanca on August 19, 1985, "that we, Christian and Muslims, must recognize with joy the religious values that we have in common, and give thanks to God for them. Both of us believe in one God."

From this faith in God springs an understanding of the human person which is virtually the same: created by God, "servant of God" (*'abd Allah*), the crowning element of the universe, steward of God's gifts, subject to the law of good and evil, called to attain to God as ultimate end. Christians and Muslims can therefore join hands, again in the words of John Paul II at Casablanca, "in building a world where God may have first place in order to aid and to save mankind."

It would be wrong, however, to think that dialogue is easy. For while it is true that dialogue with Muslims, as indeed with Jews, is based on the common platform of biblical theism, it should not be forgotten that the image of God and connected values have been handed down to Christians and Muslims respectively through the historical mediation of Jesus and Muhammad, as to Jews through that of Moses. The spiritual outlook of Jesus is profoundly different from that of Muhammad. Consequently the historical mediations of the founders stamp Islam and Christianity with characteristics which remain irreducible despite common spiritual structures. For this reason Christians who engage in dialogue often feel frustrated at the ambiguity of Islamic terminology, and Muslims have the same experience in dealing with Christians. Basic terms and concepts, such as faith, revelation, prophets, law, sacred books, freedom, human rights, ethics, and salvation, have different meanings and resonance in Christian and Muslim contexts. Hence there is a constant risk of misunderstanding and of reaching a point of incommunicability.

This vital aspect of dialogue was not passed over by the Pope in his Casablanca address. He stated quite simply and confidently:

> Loyalty demands also that we should recognize and respect our differences. Obviously the most fundamental is the view that we hold on the person and work of Jesus of Nazareth . . . whom Christians recognize and proclaim as Lord and Savior. These are important differences, which we can accept with humility and respect, in mutual tolerance; there is a mystery there on which, I am certain, God will one day enlighten us.

In this spirit of confident surrender to the mystery of God, Father of all believers, steps can be taken, with sincerity and clarity, along the path of dialogue. This book will be a help along the way. Readers will be grateful to the author, Fr. Borrmans, for his guidance, and to Dr. Marston Speight, faculty member of the Duncan Black MacDonald Center for the Study of Islam and Christian-Muslim Relations of Hartford Seminary (U.S.A.), for having so ably provided this English translation.

Rt. Rev. Pietro Rossano
Rector of the Pontifical Lateran University
Auxiliary Bishop of Rome for Cultural Affairs

Preface to the English Translation

I am happy to present the English translation of *Orientations pour un Dialogue entre Chrétiens et Musulmans.* Many translations of this book have already appeared: German, Dutch, Arabic, Turkish, Italian. An English version has long been awaited.

These *Guidelines,* first published in French in 1981, were written by Fr. Maurice Borrmans, professor at the Pontifical Institute of Arabic and Islamic Studies in Rome, on behalf of the Secretariat for Non-Christians, now known as the Pontifical Council for Interreligious Dialogue. Fr. Borrmans, a specialist in the field of Islamic law, lived for twenty years in North Africa before coming to Rome in 1964. Since then he has traveled widely throughout the Islamic world, giving courses in Islam, engaging in pastoral work in Christian communities, participating in scientific conferences and in dialogue meetings. He was thus eminently suited to draw up these *Guidelines.* He was moreover able to make use of the suggestions and comments of a group of Consultors of the Secretariat.

The purpose of the *Guidelines* is to provide a basic knowledge of Islamic beliefs and practices so that Christians may be better prepared to engage in dialogue with Muslims. Other essential aspects are also studied: the ideas of Muslims about Christianity and Christians, the possibilities of theological convergence, and areas of possible collaboration.

In the Catholic Church, dialogue, in the spirit of the Second Vatican Council, has been untiringly supported and encouraged by the teaching and the example of Pope Paul VI and Pope John Paul II. The visit of the latter to Morocco in August 1985, and the World Day of Prayer for Peace in Assisi on October 27, 1986, are outstanding examples of this commitment to dialogue.

Increased contact with Muslims in many countries, indeed in almost all parts of the world, makes serious reflection on the part of Christians ever more necessary. These *Guidelines* will, I am sure, prove extremely useful for this purpose. In the name of the Pontifical Council for Interreligious Dialogue I heartily recommend them.

Francis Cardinal Arinze, President
Pontifical Council for Interreligious Dialogue

Preface to the 1981 Edition

It is with great pleasure that the Secretariat for Non-Christians presents this new edition of *Guidelines for Dialogue between Christians and Muslims.*

The first edition of this book was published in 1970, following the initiative of the Second Vatican Council. It gave background material and practical suggestions to encourage dialogue between Christians and Muslims.

That initiative evidently filled a widely felt need, since the first edition sold out quickly. Translations into several languages were made in response to requests received by the Secretariat.

As the years have passed we have deepened our reflection on dialogue. Practical experience has given us a better grasp of various situations. Lessons of the past have helped us to understand the present. Prayer has given us a purer view, a larger heart and a stronger thirst for truth. We could not simply reprint in 1980 the pages that were written in 1970. A note added to the introduction of this book gives some idea of the intensive work that went into the production of this small volume. It has turned out to be a completely revised and corrected edition. Readers of the first edition will do well to take note of this fact.

Even as was the case with the first, the new edition makes no claim to be definitive. Every dialogue has its own dynamics. Those who take part in honest exchanges of opinion and friendly cooperation with others are themselves transformed by the mutual benefit of such activity. They are able to recognize errors and to envisage perspectives of which they would not have previously dreamed.

So, these *Guidelines,* first published in 1981 in French, are presented to their readers in the hope that they will provide new encouragement for those engaged in Christian-Muslim relations.

Today ease of communication and the multiplying of opportunities to bring people together make it possible for both good and evil influences to be spread rapidly. It is to be hoped that those who believe in the One, All-Powerful and All-Merciful God will take concerted advantage of this situation for the benefit of all.

Jean Jadot, Pro-President
Secretariat for Non-Christians

Introduction

The world in which we live today consists of an amazing multiplicity of ideologies, cultures and religions. People must live together even if they are very different from each other. Will they be able to go beyond mere coexistence or tolerance, and try to get to know one another at a deeper level of community life? Even if they concede the need to maintain peaceable relations of a sort with people who are different from themselves, thus contributing to a measure of social harmony, this will be an extremely precarious state of affairs as long as they hold back from full appreciation of one another's uniqueness.

The fact is that differences between peoples have often been the cause of painful conflicts and they remain today a constant source of discord. Men and women of good will would like, however, to discuss the possibilities of meeting together and of living happily even in the diversity of their religious traditions. Without ever forgetting the requirements of truth and the unity of God's purpose for humanity, can believers entertain the possibility that this diversity possesses some positive aspects, and that it is not wholly without meaning? Only an intense and courageous dialogue among Muslims, Jews and Christians can bring these believers, with their respective loyalty to the "faith of Abraham," to determine the reasons for their differences and the ways in which they agree.

There are no doubt many other people who consider themselves believers, even monotheists, but without reference to the biblical message. It is also possible and needful to develop cooperation with them and to seek for agreement. However, since this book is addressed mainly to Christians, especially Catholics, and since it presupposes that they will be in relationship with Muslims of all points of view, we have deemed it advisable to use the term "believers" to designate all those who hold explicitly to the "faith of Abraham."

As far as the believers of Islam and the followers of Jesus are concerned, they are called upon to consider the various forms their life together has taken through centuries of eventful history. God invites them now to draw the lessons from their history which will help them to realize that by following the path of dialogue they will be able to give a better witness and to cooperate peaceably in service to God and humanity.

These chapters have been written to help Christians, especially Catholics, since the Second Vatican Council asked them to rediscover the apostolic requirements of an open dialogue in which the participants fully accept each other and share together both the content of their faith and the values of their tradition. Christians and Muslims find themselves today in a great variety of historical situations and personal circumstances, which means that dialogue, even though it has always existed, is seen now in new perspective. These pages contain brief discussions and suggestions for Christians concerning the multiple dimensions of their present-day dialogue with Muslims.

Many people talk about dialogue without a good understanding of its requirements and its methods. It has nothing to do with the extremes, either of a facile syncretism which would make all religions alike, or an uncompromising polemic which would deny that different religions can ever meet each other. Dialogue is, rather, a daring adventure engaged in by people desiring mutual enrichment from their different ways, fellowship in sharing common values and openness to whatever way the Lord might speak to them in the intimacy of their conscience. Certainly Christians and Muslims have divergent ideas as to what is involved in their meeting together. This is to be expected since they are different. This book will try to bring them together a little by helping the Christians to develop a spirit of dialogue marked with respect and love as well as with intelligence and understanding. Christians who want to be faithful to the Gospel cannot be indifferent to a true encounter with those who, although they do not have the same faith, are nevertheless seeking to honor God as they proceed on their own particular way toward Him. Without any concession whatever to doctrinal rigidity on the one hand, or to a polemical spirit on the other, Christians must explore, under the Spirit's guidance, any possible ways of convergence between themselves and Muslims, who may well be their relatives, their neighbors or their friends. In the following chapters will be found some friendly suggestions on how to go as far as possible in the way of peaceable encounter and sharing.

These *Guidelines* conform to the vision of dialogue here presented, so they are intended only for those who have made the Gospel their rule and ideal. Without any syncretism we have constantly emphasized the common values which should unite Muslims and Christians at all levels both of their experience with God and of their service to humanity. Also we have tried to deal in a clear and calm way with some of the most difficult aspects of dialogue. These pages should be read and understood in a generous spirit of faith, hope and charity. Dialogue seeks essentially a better understanding of one another, a deepening of one's faith and religious awareness, a more zealous and single-minded quest for the will of God and conversion to the Lord, the One who calls us all into question, who pardons and who transforms. Therefore dialogue cannot have as its purpose the will to "convert" other persons to one's own religion at any price or to try to make them doubt the faith in which they were raised. On the contrary, believers in dialogue engage in a holy "spiritual emulation" in which they "vie one with another in good works" (Qur'an 5:48), that is, they seek to help each other "surpass themselves," to become more closely conformed to the path which the Lord has indicated to them and thus draw closer to Him in the practice of active goodness.

The present text follows closely the outline of the previous one, also entitled *Guidelines for Dialogue between Christians and Muslims,* and was inspired by the teachings of the last Council. We have felt that it is appropriate first of all to describe "the partners in dialogue" (Chapter One), then to point out "the places and the paths of dialogue" (Chapter Two), so that its spirit and its method might be made clear on the two levels of human encounter and the fellowship of believers. Consequently Christians should feel led to "recognize the values of others" (Chapter Three), with intellectual honesty and spiritual generosity. At the same time discernment and prudence allow them to "deal with present obstacles" (Chapter Four) which need to be removed or reduced, or at least recognized, in order to give dialogue a chance to succeed. Possibilities for success are described in "areas of cooperation" (Chapter Five) and "potential areas of religious agreement" (Chapter Six), where Christians and Muslims are challenged with proposals for practical cooperation both in the area of concrete action and through religious research in the two traditions so as to develop a spirituality that is open to mutual enrichment.

Such are the perspectives according to which this book has been written. We have taken into account the advice of many people who are already engaged in dialogue, and we have tried to foresee the expectations and needs of Christians and Muslims who are called upon to dialogue. These are *Guidelines* only, that is, brief proposals addressed to Christian readers concerning a better dialogue with Muslims. It is up to the readers to apply the principles herein enunciated, in fellowship with their local Church and in awareness of their particular circumstances. They should also adapt the *Guidelines* depending upon the persons with whom they form friendships, as well as upon the nature of their encounters. In addition, readers should not forget to invoke the Spirit of God, because it is only through His constant help that these new *Guidelines* have been written.

NOTE

In 1979–80 Father Maurice Borrmans wrote the original draft of this book, collaborating closely with Father Ary Roest Crollius. Then it was carefully studied and criticized by Monsignor Pietro Rossano (Rome), Brother Martin Sabanegh (deceased) (Rome), Father Joseph Cuoq (deceased) (Tunis), Fathers Andre Ferre (Rome), Khalil Samir (Rome), and other specialists. Then the manuscript was reduced to two-thirds of its original length and rearranged by the two authors previously mentioned. It was again submitted for critical analysis, this time to Monsignor Pietro Rossano, Monsignor Henri Teissier (then coadjutor to the Archbishop of Algiers), Father Martin Sabanegh (deceased), Professor Mohammed Talbi (Tunis), Fathers Robert Caspar (Monastir, Tunisia), André Ferré, Jacques Jomier (Cairo, Egypt), Michel Lelong (Paris and Tunis), and Christian W. Troll (New Delhi, India). The text here presented was put into final form by Father Maurice Borrmans, in close cooperation with Father Ary Roest Crollius, taking into account all of the remarks and suggestions which the aforementioned experts provided.

For the English translation of the Bible the Revised Standard Version has been followed, and for the English translation of the Qur'an, the version of Mohammad M. Pickthall (New American Library, n.d.) as often as possible. The Notes have been adapted and amplified by the translator for English readers.

Chapter One
The Partners in Dialogue

Christians and Muslims find themselves nearly everywhere living together in a world that moves painfully toward unity. Whether deliberately or not they are collaborating for human progress, working together for the well-being of all, side by side with many people, believers and unbelievers, those who belong to the great historic religions, to recent religious movements and to modern ideologies. Whereas in former times there was a fairly clear division of the world into Muslim countries, Christian ones and others, that is no longer the case, since Christian communities are found everywhere, be they ancient or modern, native or foreign, minority or majority, and since Muslim communities have been strongly implanted in Western Europe and in America, outside the countries that Islam has specially marked with its religious and cultural influence. So it is in a new historical and geographical framework, expanded to the scale of the planet itself, that Muslims and Christians are called upon to develop their relations and to dialogue, all the while taking into account the great variety of local cultural, political and economic settings.[1]

From its very beginning as an opposition movement to Meccan polytheism on the Arabian peninsula, Islam considered itself as a close or distant relative of the Judaism which was practiced in Yathrib (Medina) and in other centers, as well as a friendly neighbor of the Christians, feeling that it, Islam, was a complement to the Monophysite communities of Yemen and Ethiopia, the Nestorian Churches of the Sassanid Empire and the Jacobites and Melkites of the Byzantine Empire. Before long, however, lines of exclusivism began to be drawn between the two communities and anathemas were pronounced. Dialogue between Muslims and Christians began dramatically at the *Mubahala*[2] of Medina (631 A.D.) (Qur'an 3:61) when the Christians of Najran submitted to the authority of the young Islamic state and accepted its pact of "protection" (*dhimma*). After that relationships between the two religious communities were nothing but a long series of political, cultural and religious confrontations in the course of which polemical debates and ideological challenges led to a thousand misunderstandings and prejudices which only increased with the passage of time. This was in spite of the efforts of certain noble figures, from one side or the other, who tried in each century to reduce the mis-comprehensions and solve the problems of relationships by a friendly spirit of coexistence and cooperation.

It should be recognized that the knowledge of Islam in Christian countries has varied according to the times and especially depending upon whether or not the Arabic language has been known. From the seventh to the eleventh centuries Muslim-Christian dialogue was mainly theological in nature, and then later it became increasingly characterized by scientific exchanges. However there has always been the political factor to interfere: Muslim conquests, reconquests by the Christians, Crusades, Ottoman expansion, the colonial enterprise, and recent struggles for independence.

The Arab Christian Orient, which played an active part in building the Arab civilization, was able to dialogue with the Muslims of the era in the persons of Melkites Theodore Abu Qurra (d. about 825), Qusta Ibn Luqa (d. about 912) and Paul of Antioch (13th century); Syrians Abu Ra'ita al-Takriti (d. about 830), Yahya Ibn 'Adi (793–874) and 'Isa Ibn Zur'a (943–1008); Nestorians Hunayn Ibn Ishaq (d. 873) and Elias of Nisibis (975–1046); and Copts Sawirus Ibn al-Muqaffa' (d. about 1000) and Al-Safi Ibn al-'Assal (thirteenth century).[3]

The Latin West was disadvantaged by its ignorance of the Arabic language, and gave much attention to works of translation. Among these was the first Latin version of the Qur'an, translated by Peter of Cluny (1146). Then Raymond Llull (1235–1315) came upon the scene, a Franciscan tertiary from Majorca, who presented an ideal of peaceable dialogue which could serve as a mediator between the two cultures and religions. The "mission" of Saint Francis to the court of the Sultan of Egypt caught the imagination of many, and we can say that Saint Thomas Aquinas (1225–74), William of Tripoli (thirteenth century) and especially Nicholas of Cusa (mid-fifteenth century) went beyond controversy to prepare, each in his own way, an encounter which would finally be respectful and genuine.[4]

It appears that, in the first stage, the Muslim-Christian dialogue of the Middle Ages was characterized by confidence in philosophical reasoning and by systematic recourse to scriptural texts. Many early personalities showed a certain sensitivity to historical realities, and, whereas in the East, Christians tended to identify Islam as one of the unhappy heresies that had arisen within Christendom, the Latins of the West seemed more aware of the Judeo-Christian elements of the Islamic religion. The motives for interest in Islam varied, ranging from that of simple witness to a concern for polemics to eschatological expectations and to papal political enterprises in Islamic territories.

In more recent times, with the European Renaissance and the glory of the Ottoman Empire, Muslim-Christian dialogue took on more of a scientific and cultural nature, inspired by philosophical rationalism. The nineteenth century saw the birth of European orientalism. It was contemporaneous with colonial expansion and with a new missionary effort by the Churches, and, after being at first their ally, it became the voice of their bad conscience and their critic. Orientalism has always tried to interpret Islam and understand Muslims by reference to the Arab-Islamic sources, if possible, and by basing its investigation on scientific criteria, although current ideologies were never without influence upon their work.

Also in modern times, thanks to certain "prophetic Christians," such as Miguel Asin y Palacios, Louis Massignon and others, the Church's regard for Islam has been renewed, and that religion is now understood, scientifically and theologically, as a monotheism which is inspired by the divine promises to Abraham. Many groups of Christians engaged in active witness have come to similar conclusions, albeit expressed in less intellectual terms, based on their diverse experiences. These groups have come from the Catholic, Protestant and Anglican branches of Christianity. All of this led up to the Second Vatican Council's *Declaration on the Relation of the Church to Non-Christian Religions* (*Nostra Aetate*) which has become, for Catholics, the "Charter of Muslim-Christian Dialogue." So, after having known centuries of theological and political polemics, and having gone through certain periods of inappropriate proselytism, relations between Christians and Muslims seem now to have entered a time of respect and understanding in which Christians, for their part, try to appreciate Muslims on the basis of the best in the latter's religious experience.

I
THE CHRISTIANS:
THEIR CHURCHES AND THEIR COMMUNITIES[5]

For a long time the Christian communities of the Arab Middle East, of the Byzantine Empire and of Western Europe were apparently the only ones to bear the responsibility for dialogue with Islam. This is no longer the case. As the recent Second Vatican Council and the various Assemblies of the World Council of Churches testify, Christians everywhere are seeking ecumenical reconciliation among themselves, and in some cases canonical communion. A part of this growing sense of worldwide responsibility is a concomitant openness to other religions, including Islam. Nevertheless since the weight of history and the geographical setting give to each situation its original stamp and so control in some measure the chances for success or failure of dialogue, it is fitting to note the distinctive circumstances, in turn, of the ancient apostolic Churches of the Middle East, the new Churches in Asia and Africa, the Christian communities in solidly Muslim countries and, finally, the populations with a Christian majority and a Muslim minority.

Today on all six continents Christians and Muslims work together at both national and international levels of economic, cultural and political life. Everywhere, too, Christian communities are called upon to establish new kinds of ties with Muslim communities, in which the two are bound together and yet each remains autonomous, complementing each other without losing their particularity. The forming and maintaining of such interfaith relations is a highly demanding enterprise, calling for special sensitivity to the Holy Spirit's guidance in orienting Church members toward openness to those of another religion.

Orthodox, Reformed and Catholic Christians tend to complement each other in their efforts to coordinate their diverse approaches to the personal and communal religious experience of Muslims. They will probably have to accept, at least for the present, the fact that they are different in the way that they look at Islam. For example, Christians who have emphasized in their thought and devotion the richness of divine transcendence, the gratuitous love of God the Father and the obedience of a childlike submission to God, such Christians will be in a better position than many to understand and appreciate the abiding values of faith and submission in Islam. On the other hand those Christians who have become very sensitive to the requirements of justice and to human rights, the rights of humanity "deified" by the redemptive work of Jesus Christ, such Christians will have difficulty in entering into the nature of the Muslim's religious experience. They will not easily grasp the main points of Islamic faith, nor will they respond quickly to its grandeur. In their double emphasis on transcendence and immanence, on the marvels of life within the divine Trinity as well as on the human condition, on both divine rights and human rights, Christians might not realize that their dialogue with Muslims will be somewhat easier if it takes the absoluteness of God as its point of departure, although it is also possible for dialogue to develop on the basis of a common involvement in service to humanity.

Within the two families of Christian spirituality, which differ only in the importance attached on the one hand to the Father's initiative in "distributing His blessings" or, on the other hand, to the solidarity of the incarnate Word with his brothers and sisters, it should be pointed out that Christians also have two very different ways of approaching interreligious dialogue. Some are inclined by temperament to see only the common ground between religions at the risk of over-emphasizing it, whereas others tend constantly to call attention to divergences, and this at the risk of making one partner a complete stranger to the spiritual experience of the other. There are those who would readily be syncretists, considering everyone to be alike, and there are others who choose to stand firm by stressing the differences, in the interest of being faithful to the gift received from God. In these distinctions cannot Christians see complementary attitudes and methods which help to make possible a richer and more authentic dialogue with Muslims than would be possible otherwise?

II
MUSLIMS IN THEIR UNITY
AND THEIR DIVERSITY[6]

Muslims today, wherever they are, are very well aware that they belong to a "mother" community, *Umma* (*umm* means mother), which forms them, nourishes them, permeates them, surrounds them, supports them and exalts them. This community is Islam, an undivided society where all members are interdependent brothers and sisters, their differences of race, language and civilization notwithstanding. Fourteen centuries of history have seen the "House of Islam" incorporate many peoples and islamize prestigious cultures in the Afro-Asiatic third world. In modern times a sizable Muslim diaspora has spread across Europe and America. The Muslim partners in dialogue today are characterized as much by their cultural environment and their national situation as they are by their faith.

Arab Muslims, although they are a minority in the Islamic world (being only twenty percent of the whole), occupy nevertheless a central place geographically, culturally and emotionally. They enjoy unmatched prestige in the Muslim world by virtue of the fact that they were the propagators of Islam during the first centuries of Muslim expansion and the fact that their language is the one in which the Qur'an was given and in which that holy Book is still recited everywhere.

Other Muslims consider that they represent forms of historical Islam just as authentic as that of the Arabs. The community of India and Pakistan, dating back to the first centuries of Islamic history, has had its own development and characteristics. The latest stage in its evolution is the contrast between the Muslims of Pakistan and Bangladesh on the one hand, and those of India on the other. The former have adopted an Islamic constitution as their national ideal, whereas the latter have accepted a model of pluralism for their society. Indonesian Muslims, whose adoption of Islam is more recent and whose culture is very distinctive, are involved in the pluralistic national ideology which has the *Pancasila*[7] as its charter. Islam in the Asiatic and Caucasian Soviet Republics has much to say about how its communities can live and develop in a Marxist and totalitarian society. Muslims in China can give a similar testimony, since they live under the same conditions.

Islam in Iran was only Arabized for a few centuries. It has seen the triumphant evolution of a particular interpretation of the Muslim tradition, taking the form of a mystical and revolutionary Shi'ism. In Turkey the modern successor of the Ottoman Empire which ruled the Mediterranean world from the fifteenth until the twentieth centuries, Islam is expressed in nationalistic and secular models. In the Balkan states, issue also of the Ottoman Empire, the Muslims are in the minority, living in Marxist pluralistic societies. The Muslim communities of black Africa represent such a variety of successive and original processes of Islamization that the continent reflects today a vast mosaic of diverse and unique symbioses between the African tradition and the Islamic religion.[8]

It is, then, in relation to their place in these socio-cultural zones of contemporary Islam that Muslim partners in dialogue meet their Christian associates. Each people has been able to retain its language and its culture, and even to integrate many religious values from its distant past into its practice of Islam. As a result there may be observed unusual ways of carrying out the ritual practices, preference expressed for certain ceremonies, particular modes of balancing the requirements of strict orthodoxy with the response to mysticism, sometimes seen in rather extreme forms, as in the brotherhoods. There is also a variety of ways in which the Islamic law is fulfilled, depending upon which legal rite is followed and upon the ethical traditions which may be particular to the population in question.

The ways of expressing faith and morality show in Islam, as in Christendom, a thousand local colorations and cultural variations, which must be taken into account as influencing dialogue. Islam in Senegal is not the same as Islam in Nigeria. Islam in Morocco is not that of Iraq, even as Italian Catholicism is not French Catholicism, nor is British Anglicanism similar to Norwegian Lutheranism. However, this multiplicity of religious, regional and national characteristics should never obscure the fact that powerful factors for unity shape Muslim communities wherever they are.

Muslims retain a deep nostalgia for the greatness of their past, when Baghdad was the center of the world and the "House of Islam" was ruled by a single caliph (or vicar of the Apostle of God). Nevertheless they attempt to live today as harmoniously as possible in their various national

and cultural settings, which divide them, and in attachment to the one
Book and one Law, which unify them. The annual participation of a
multitude of pilgrims, ever growing larger, in the ceremonies of pilgrimage (*hajj*) to Mecca is both a marvelous symbol and a tangible sign of the
unity which brings Muslim men and women together (the latter constitute now nearly a third of the pilgrims). The gathering in Mecca has been
facilitated by the advances in air travel and by modernization of the facili-
ties at the pilgrimage sites. On pilgrimage Muslims transcend their ethnic,
linguistic, economic and political diversity, because there "believers are
naught else than brothers," as the Qur'an itself affirms (49:10). Upon such
occasions Muslims are naturally reminded of how transitory are the
barriers of political boundaries and ideological divisions. Coming from
such a "unifying retreat" as the pilgrimage, they renew their longing to see
Muslim countries unite to form on the earth "the Abode of Peace," according to the laws ordained by the God "who gathers together" (*Al-
Jami'*) and "who guides" (*Al-Hadi*).

It is because the holy Book was given in Arabic and because it can
only be understood, interpreted and recited in its original language that
the Arab civilization constituted the essential framework of the whole
Islamic edifice. Everyone knows how much such diverse languages as
Indonesian, Urdu, Persian, Turkish, Swahili and Wolof owe to the Arabic
language for their religious vocabulary, and even that of jurisprudence,
culture, politics and administration. So no one can claim to understand
the Qur'an, know the Tradition (*Sunna*), study theology (*Kalam*) and
interpret the Law (*Shari'a*) without first learning the language of the Arabs and grasping the essential elements of their civilization. Formerly, for
several centuries the Arab and Persian cultures provided, in the Middle
East, in Africa and in Asia, a strong factor for holding peoples together,
and even for attracting others to join them, since they transmitted a genuine universalism and a true humanism, creating thus among very
diverse peoples bonds of political, religious and cultural unity. Some
Muslims wish that today Islamic cultures would recover that same function and achieve the same success, going beyond linguistic and ideological
boundaries.

The concern for unity among contemporary Muslims has given rise
to quite a few organizations of which Christians should be aware. In fact
since the abolition of the Ottoman caliphate by Kemal Ataturk (March 3,
1924) there have been many efforts to reestablish the vicarial office for the
guidance of the religious community. The caliph, vicar of the Prophet, has
always been considered as the keeper of unity, at least among Sunnis.
When the first Panislamic congresses failed to achieve results in this regard, the Arab League, founded in 1945, sought a solution to the problem.

But that body was too much marked by its Arab character to be useful in the search for unity. Its role in that area was quickly taken up by new Panislamic congresses. As a result of those efforts and under the aegis of the Arab Summit meetings, there was held in Rabat in September 1969, soon after the burning of the Al-Aqsa Mosque in Jerusalem, the first Summit meeting of the Conference of Islamic Countries. Since then these Summit meetings are held each year in first one and then another capital city, bringing together about fifty government ministers and heads of state to coordinate their various enterprises in the areas of politics, economics, religion and culture. Similarly, the Muslim World League was begun in Mecca, in May 1962, destined quickly to become an international organization endowed with religious and cultural responsibilities for the purpose of helping Muslim communities everywhere in their practices of worship, their education and in fulfilling their missionary duty (*da'wa*). Thus when such diverse organizations join forces with the Islamic Development Bank and the Islamic Solidarity Fund, Muslims of today can be more assured of the future success of their quest for unity, and take satisfaction in that they are being more faithful to the command of God: "And hold fast, all of you together, to the cable of Allah, and do not separate" (Qur'an 3:103).

However, Muslims are far from being agreed on how to interpret their history, conceive of their unity, practice their worship or clarify their law. Ever since the beginning the exercise of personal interpretation (*ijtihad*) has made it possible for different religious temperaments to express themselves and to live together in recognition that "difference of opinions is a mercy," as a hadith affirms. Muslims are in large majority Sunnis, and this means that they recognize the legitimacy of the first four caliphs (Abu Bakr, 'Umar, 'Uthman and 'Ali). Sunnis hold strictly to the Qur'an and the Tradition (*Sunna*) of the Prophet, and are also very careful to follow the unanimous counsel (*ijma'*) of the community as expressed by the scholars of Islam, who have "the power to bind and to loosen." At the same time, it is well known that Sunnis practice a certain degree of diversity within the four different schools of law which they have formed (Hanafites, Malikites, Shafi'ites and Hanbalites).

The Shi'ites (8.75 percent of the Islamic world population) are found in Iran, Iraq, India and Lebanon. Their distinctive Muslim religious experience consists of a close solidarity with 'Ali, the cousin and son-in-law of Muhammad, and with the legitimate successors (*Imams*) of that sole heir of the prophetic charisma of the founder of Islam. Most of the partisans of 'Ali (this is the meaning of the word *shi'a*, party) believe that twelve

Imams have thus watched over the destiny of the Muslim community, and they await the return of the "hidden" Imam. Certain groups have had their moments of glory in the course of history, such as the Fatimids of the tenth and eleventh centuries. Many today are scattered into active minority communities, such as the Druses of Lebanon and Syria, whose practice includes initiatory rites, and the followers of Agha Khan, or Nizarite Ismailians (especially in Pakistan, India and East Africa), who attribute superhuman qualities to their Imam.

The Kharijites (0.25 percent of the world population of Muslims), found in Oman, Zanzibar and in a few places in North Africa, represent a strict and cultured expression of Islam based on an historic refusal of any compromise between 'Ali and his adversaries. The Kharijites believe that only the most devout of Muslims is worthy to assume the leadership of the community.

Such are the important variations in Islamic orthodoxy, according to which the differences between Sunnis, Shi'ites and Kharijites seem to be more on the questions of choosing the leaders of the Islamic community and insuring their succession than on essential matters of doctrine, worship and ethics. Also within Sunnism of the present era there are new ways of understanding the religion which should be noted here. The Wahhabis of Arabia, whose reform movement dates from the end of the eighteenth century, represent today a kind of Muslim puritanism which is all-pervading and which enjoys the favor of the Saudi Arabian state. Elsewhere many other reformers have appeared, as, for example, Mohammed 'Abduh (1849–1905) in Egypt and Al-Mawdudi (1903–79) in Pakistan. These leaders have sought to lead Sunni Islam back to the purity of its origins. The movement of the Muslim Brotherhood, originating in Egypt with Hasan al-Banna (1906–49) and thereafter very active in many regions, often appears as a political reform movement with a fundamentalist stamp, marked by a decisive rejection of the West. The *Tablighi Jama'at,* of Indian origin and inspired by Maulana Mohammed Ilyas, seeks reform within the Islamic religious community.

Just as in the Christian world, the "House of Islam" has had and has yet the phenomenon of sects. It is important to distinguish these from the main branches of Islam which we have just described. There are the Baha'is, an international syncretistic movement based on an Islamic pattern, and the Ahmadis, especially those of the Qadyan group in India, who constitute a syncretistic and missionary tendency often contested by local Sunni communities. Just as Christians today do their best to bring about ecumenical reconciliation between brothers and sisters in Jesus Christ, so they should be careful not to call undue attention to the divergences and divisions among their Muslim associates.

The Muslim partners in dialogue are found within this vast framework of Islamic unity with its world of religious, ethnic, linguistic and political diversity. There was a time when many sought to follow Western European or American models of economic development and humanistic ideology; and some still do. There followed a time when a large number of Muslims turned readily to the progressive and efficacious models of contemporary Marxism, be they Soviet or Yugoslav; and quite a few are still following them. Finally has come a time, it seems, when most desire to create new models of their own, based on national or Islamic authenticity and for the purpose of carrying out agricultural, cultural and industrial revolutions. From all of this there results a great diversity of opinions, attitudes and behaviors, which certainly influences the possibilities that exist for Muslim-Christian dialogue. For this reason it is perhaps useful to try to describe certain broad types of contemporary Muslims, even if we understand that in reality it is possible to belong to several types simultaneously.

1. Muslims of the Working Class

Whether they belong to the rural masses of the developing countries or to the new world of workers in the modern economy, Muslims of the working class have a common concern to follow the traditional, communal faith and practice of Islam, in which are exemplified many of the religious values of the "Biblical believer." In their faithfulness to God and to their ancestors, their attachment to ceremonies and customs, their natural conservatism in family and social life, these persons articulate their religious experience in pithy formulations drawing upon Qur'an verses and prophetic hadith. Often they still take part in religious brotherhoods in which they are given religious training, as well as guidance in the affairs of social, political and even economic life. Those of the large number who have emigrated for work in other Muslim countries, Europe or America are enduring difficult situations of displacement or social disintegration. Sometimes, especially when they are young, they join the laboring classes where they share in the aspirations and struggles of the labor movement; but they never forget the religious values of their homeland, and they are eager to take part in any useful, consistent effort to help them resettle in religious communities provided with places of worship and religious education.

Whether they come from traditional environments or from the modern world, these numerous "silent" Muslims will often be the first partners in dialogue. They are always sensitive to the values of faith, prayer, work, gratitude, hospitality, generosity, patience in suffering and acceptance of death. By virtue of some of their recent experiences, they are also increasingly sensitive to the values of human dignity, freedom, equality and brotherhood, as well as to the message of the Beatitudes. Thus we can expect them to take part in dialogue, using their particular manner of expression, a dialogue which will not be only companionship at work or in the neighborhood, but which will consist of faith lived, suffering borne, friendship sought and death transcended.

2. Muslims with Religious Training, whether Traditional or Reformist

These are the faithful heirs of the ancients who developed and transmitted classical Muslim theology as well as the varied literary creations of the Arabic and Persian languages. They are the Muslim intellectuals, trained in Arabic, Persian or Urdu, to mention only the most important languages; and today they consider themselves to be the natural interpreters, in explicit detail, of Islam as lived by the masses of uneducated believers. Against the background of the ancient Islamic universities, such as the one in Cairo (Al-Azhar) and under the influence of new Islamic centers being developed everywhere, they transmit to the modern generation Islam's patrimony of exegesis, theology, jurisprudence and mysticism. Sometimes this entails an effort at reinterpretation, either according to the classical methods of the law schools, or by carefully going back to the Qur'an and *Sunna* as sole sources for legitimate change. These persons are authentic contemporaneous witnesses of the age-long activities of spiritual research, philosophical reflection, juridical elaboration and daring mystical quests which occupied the lives of multitudes in the past and whose records fill the libraries. No one can say how deeply this Islamic culture, be it Arab, Persian or Urdu, has marked the world of Muslims. Without doubt it is one of the principal components of that world's present identity, and it constitutes one of the most original manifestations of universal religious culture.

The traditionalists prefer to express their religious experience in the language of the great masters of classical Muslim thought, judging that there is no need, or scarcely any need, to take into account the modern developments of textual criticism, of the social sciences and of religious psychology. Sometimes they even use the vocabulary of Muslim mysticism to reveal the richness of their inner life. The reformists are more concerned to prove that Islam can be reconciled with the rationality of the modern world, so they want to use scientific methods. To them, faith and reason are best harmonized by reference to the basic sources of Muslim thought. They often criticize what they consider to be blameworthy innovations of the past, refusing even to accept the developments of Muslim mysticism, especially as it was transmitted by the religious brotherhoods.

3. Modernist Muslims, Those Having Two Cultures

There are many Muslims who, besides their national culture and Islamic background, have fully adopted another culture, be it European or American, Eastern or Western. They have done this for political, economic or technological reasons, persuaded that they can take on the values, methods and languages of the new culture without giving up their national and Islamic authenticity. They may be secular-minded, even sympathetic with Marxism, rationalistic or agnostic, so that they appear to be alienated from Islam. This is not the case, however, for they manifest an acute "Islamic consciousness." They are strong supporters of complete personal freedom of interpretation (*ijtihad*) and of human rights as seen by the modern world. To them the Quranic message can be reduced to certain broad principles and the Muslim tradition to some simple practices whose application and expression need to be renewed according to the times and the circumstances. These Muslims are government officials, intellectuals or technicians, and in their own experience they feel constrained to balance traditional values with modern ones, choosing from whichever of them seem appropriate, depending on personal needs, national ideology and the practical requirements of their people.

In their position as agents for the transformation of their society, and at the same time as answerable to their own conscience, they feel more keenly than most the cultural gap that exists between the classical expression of religion and the demands of the contemporary world. In practice they tend to separate the temporal from the spiritual, favoring confessional pluralism and egalitarianism, where circumstances permit. They are courageous social reformers, even in such matters as family law. In a word these persons judge the quality of faith by the deeds that it produces and assess a religion according to the values which it inculcates among the masses of believers.

The modernist Muslims, with their particular kind of humanism, have more opportunity than most to meet Christians and other people of good will on the level of their involvement in social concerns, such as human rights; freedom of thought, faith and expression; birth control and family welfare; struggle against underdevelopment; technological progress; etc. In their way they witness that Islam stands as much for generous action and untiring devotion as it does for the building of a more just and humane society.

4. Muslim Fundamentalists or Literalists

There exist Muslims today who would like to see Islam applied to all parts of public and private life, since they are convinced that the Law revealed in the Qur'an is in every detail part of the perfect divine will for human society. They are custodians of Arab, Persian or Urdu culture, partially renewed, but still largely dependent upon classical formulations of theology and law. In their view most of the evils afflicting Muslim societies today are due to their unfaithfulness to the original design of Mecca and Medina. In their concern for the strict observance of worship and for the correct Islamic organization of life they are resolved to see the Law of God applied without compromise. Trying to bring Islam back to its essential foundations (Qur'an, Tradition and Law) they would insist on reviving institutions thought by some to be outmoded, such as the "legal status of a protected minority" (*dhimmi*) for their Jewish and Christian fellow citizens, and the corporal criminal punishments prescribed by the Qur'an. At the same time they are careful to emphasize the necessity for social justice in behalf of the poor.

Christians interested in dialogue will be led occasionally to meet Muslims of this tendency, and exchanges or cooperation with them will sometimes not be easy. They are sure of themselves and free of all complexes. Christian fundamentalists are somewhat like them in their zeal for God and their loyalty to His Law, qualities which in themselves command respect. In spite of the bluntness with which the encounter may take place, Muslim fundamentalists are perhaps better able than some to recognize and to appreciate the logic of Christian discourse and action.

Christians and Muslims experience together the diversity of situations that have just been described. In fact both are called upon to develop dialogue and cooperation in societies that are more and more interdependent and pluralistic. This can be the source of unexpected blessings or the cause of additional tension. In the meantime the modern world is present with its mass media, its ever more intrusive consumer goods, its advanced technology, its imperious ideologies and its "values," or "non-values." That world seems to challenge and defy all believers alike as it pushes for efficiency, extols practical materialism and seeks to satisfy all the desires of modern humanity. Are not religions accused of having divided the human race, alienated the masses and crushed the spirit? Capitalism and

Marxism in their practice, even as rationalist philosophy and the social sciences, all call into question the faith, morality and hope for the world that religions provide, as they remain faithful to their original message. Does not all of this constitute a massive challenge by which "modernity" summons all believers to renew their discourse, their strategies for action and their witness?

Numbers of believers think that inter-communication, the intermingling of peoples and the progressive leveling of social conditions are playing an irresistible role, even in diverse circumstances, toward unifying cultures, ways of thinking and spiritual experiences. Is this going to take place in an atmosphere of respect for all communities, in the harmonious complementarity of their various contributions to the whole, and in a spirit of openness coupled with authenticity, *or* will it take place in an atmosphere of worldwide collectivization in which individuals are surrendered defenseless to new idols of technocracy, productivity and consumerism? Must not Muslims and Christians who believe in dialogue make very clear how "the right to be different" can be reconciled with mutual understanding and collaboration at all levels of human endeavor, whether spiritual or material? Partisans of "modernity" have henceforth the possibility of continuing to evolve or, instead, of degenerating into sterile uniformity. Should not believers all together proclaim to them, in relevant terms, the marvels of the cosmos, the dignity of humankind and the greatness of God? Many see here, with good reason, the threefold perspective of any true dialogue.

It was in just such a perspective that the Second Vatican Council felt constrained to speak in the Preamble to its "Declaration on the Relation of the Church to Non-Christian Religions" (*Nostra Aetate*). "In our time," it says, "when every day men are being drawn closer together, and the ties between various peoples are being multiplied, the Church is giving deeper study . . . in this document to what human beings have in common and to what promotes fellowship among them. For all peoples comprise a single community, and have a single origin. . . . One also is their final goal: God. His providence, His manifestations of goodness, and His saving designs extend to all men." The text adds the following, as if to make clear what is at stake in dialogue: "Men look to the various religions for answers to those profound mysteries of the human condition which, today, even as in olden times, deeply stir the human heart: What is a man? What is the meaning and the purpose of our life? What is goodness, what is sin? What gives rise to our sorrows and to what intent? Where lies the path to true happiness? What is the truth about death, judgment and retribution beyond the grave? What, finally, is that ultimate and unutter-

able mystery which engulfs our being, and whence we take our rise, and
whither our journey leads us?" (*Nostra Aetate, No. 1*).[9]

Notes

1. For an account of Christian-Muslim relations in history, see J. Waardenburg, *L'Islam
dans le Miroir de l'Occident,* Paris, Mouton, 1963; R. Southern, *Western Views of Islam in
the Middle Ages,* Harvard, 1962; N. Daniel, *Islam and the West,* Edinburgh, 1960; H. Djaït,
Europe and Islam, Univ. of California, 1985; and the detailed bibliography contained in
Islamochristiana, 1975–1981 (see Bibliography).
2. For the early days of Islam, see W.M. Watt, *Muhammad at Medina* (see Bibliography);
for *dhimma,* see *Encyclopaedia of Islam,* 2nd ed.
3. See R. Southern, *Western Views . . .* and D. Sahas, *John of Damascus on Islam,* Leiden,
1972.
4. See J. Kritzeck, *Peter the Venerable and Islam,* Princeton, 1964.
5. For the Eastern Churches, a brief history and account of the more recent situation, see
A.J. Arberry (ed.), *Religion in the Middle East,* 2 vols. Cambridge, 1969; and further: P.
Rondot, *Les Chrétiens d'Orient,* Paris, Peyronnet, 1955; J. Hajjar, *Les Chrétiens Uniates du
Proche-Orient,* Paris, Seuil, 1962; J. Corbon, *L'Eglise des Arabes,* Paris, Cerf, 1975.
6. See works listed in the Bibliography, especially H.A.R. Gibb, *Modern Trends,* and
W.C. Smith, *Islam in Modern History.* See further: J.M. Cuoq, *Les Musulmans en Afrique,*
Paris, Maisonneuve et Larose, 1975; M. Arkoun and L. Gardet, *L'Islam: Hier, Demain,*
Paris, Buchet/Chastel, 1978.
7. According to the *Encyclopedia of Asian History,* New York, Charles Scribner's Sons,
1988, Pancasila is "the Indonesia state ideology to which all organizations in the country
must adhere." This ideology calls for (1) belief in one supreme deity, (2) a just and civilized
society, (3) national unity, (4) the rule of the people guided wisely through consultation and
representation, and (5) social justice for all Indonesian people.
8. See the specialized works by J.S. Trimingham on Africa (listed in Bibliography).
9. *The Documents of Vatican II,* ed. by Walter M. Abbott, S.J., New York, Guild Press,
1966. Further citations from the documents of the Council will be drawn from this source
(tr.).

Chapter Two
Places and Paths of Dialogue

Even if the word dialogue is too much in vogue these days, and easy to misunderstand, so that some people prefer to use, instead of it, words such as sharing or encounter, we use it here to express a way of living which rejects solitude, shows concern for other persons and believes that relationships with others are part of what makes up being a person. Every earnest, open-hearted believer should have a deep desire for dialogue. In fact, for Christians dialogue has a very long tradition, going back to Jesus Christ Himself. Although He was sent first of all to "the lost sheep of the House of Israel," He always sought to go beyond the barriers of social class, politics or religion. He spoke with the Samaritan woman; He listened to the Syrophoenician woman; He admired the faith of the Roman centurion, commended the repentance of the "men of Nineveh" and the wisdom of "the Queen of the South." Therefore, this word of Peter, the chief of His apostles, is applicable still to Christians today: "Always be prepared to make a defense to any who calls you to account for the hope that is in you, yet do it with gentleness and reverence; and keep your conscience clear" (I Peter 3:15–16).

Muslims, for their part, know that their Book has encouraged them from the beginning to practice dialogue with the believers who were their associates: "Dispute not with the People of the Book save in the fairer manner" (Qur'an 29:46). The Prophet himself was told, "Call thou (people) to the way of thy Lord with wisdom and good admonition and dispute with them in the better way" (Qur'an 16:125).

As concerns the Church, the Second Vatican Council has this exhortation: "prudently and lovingly, through dialogue and collaboration with the followers of other religions, and in witness of Christian faith and life, acknowledge, preserve and promote the spiritual and moral goods found among these men, as well as the values in their society and culture" (*Nostra Aetate,* No. 2).

It should be remembered, however, that dialogue between Christians and Muslims does not always develop in the same way, nor are the criteria for it uniform in every time and place. Those who seek to draw upon their rich scriptural resources, their traditions, as well as their ascetic and mysti-

cal heritage, know well that these elements from the past are deeply influenced by modern social, political, ethical, ideological and cultural factors. All that will be said in this chapter about places and paths, theology
and the spiritual demands of dialogue is addressed mainly to Christians.
The Muslim partners are not expected to assume responsibility for these
ideas on the subject, since they are completely free to consider dialogue as
they please. Then as the result of mutual consultation and honest cooperation, the two parties should be able to spell out the requirements of dialogue in their particular situation.

I
PLACES AND TIMES[1]

Here we are dealing with the dialogue of life, at all of its levels, and in
all of its parts. We cannot restrict the encounter between Christians and
Muslims to circles of specialists or to visits by the leaders of communities.
Dialogue includes all aspects of life and can be found in every place where
Muslims and Christians live and work together, love, suffer, and die. In
fact the distinctiveness of dialogue is not found in its purpose, but in a
pattern of behavior, by which other persons are welcomed, their speech is
carefully heard and the fact of their difference accepted. To behave in that
way, we do not have to be great scholars or theologians, nor even to be
advanced in the ways of holy living. It is enough to be people of faith and
hope, of good will and practical charity. In that way all are called to
dialogue, since all are taught by God and confronted by His Spirit. Does
not the Holy Spirit often intervene in our lives by the example or the
words of others, even as occurred on the road to Jericho to a certain
injured man, to whom care was given, not by the priest or the Levite, but
by the "good Samaritan"?

First of all dialogue takes place in family relationships, where Christians and Muslims belong to the same family either by blood ties or by
virtue of an interfaith marriage. Likewise at work Muslims and Christians
are called upon, even required, to meet side by side at their daily toil,
sharing the same skills of craftsmanship or the same modern technology.
Who can ever say how deep will be the dialogue of two companions at
work, or of a nurse with her patient, or even of a government official with
the citizen who applies to him or her for some service? In many places the
struggle against underdevelopment mobilizes Christians and Muslims
alike, autochthones and foreigners, to unite in labor movements, for example, or in other ideological campaigns, based on commonly held economic and political principles. Such cooperative efforts, having as their

goal the values of economic justice and the common good, are they not opportunities for a dialogue of faith between Christians and Muslims, whether on the national level or the international (the United Nations Organization, for example)? We may call this the dialogue of professional, economic and political values.

When Muslims and Christians study together, at whatever level of education, or take part in teaching anywhere in the instructional process, they have an opportunity to undertake a basic, practical dialogue around the culture which they are called upon to understand, interpret and transmit to others. At another stage, those who have the privilege of acting creatively to renew or to transform their culture will want to integrate into such an effort the religious perspective which their faith inspires. Thus, whether in scientific research or literary production or philosophical inquiry, Muslims and Christians have the opportunity of showing how their religious humanism is capable of enriching the achievements of human intelligence and contributing to the beneficial interaction of cultures.

Finally, there is a more specifically religious level where dialogue between believers has as its purpose the providing of momentum to the exchanges described above, helping them to achieve their maximum development. At this level the partners share explicitly their respective ways of approaching God. Indeed, we can never be satisfied with dialogue in which specifically religious matters are avoided, either out of apprehension or as a matter of principle. This specifically religious sharing is the natural outcome of the exchanges previously mentioned, especially if the partners are purposeful about a "dialogue of life between believers." Whatever may be the various ways of expression, or the recognized divergence in substance, such an exchange on the level of faith helps both partners to appreciate better their common heritage as they proceed toward God, and to perceive more clearly what are the important questions which await an answer from Him. This is, then, a sharing of the values of faith and can become a "dialogue of salvation," as the participants face the ineffable mystery of God.

Besides the various places of dialogue where believers are called upon to share with their brothers and sisters of other religious traditions, there are also favorable times and special events when those who take part readily set aside their distinctiveness to have fellowship together in the mutual awareness of common values. This is no doubt the case at the great turning points of life, such as birth, marriage, suffering, and death. Also festivals and holidays celebrated mutually by sending greetings, making visits and giving gifts can be an effective means for bringing people together and for regular dialogue. Christians and Muslims will demonstrate their attachment to the ideal of dialogue by taking full advantage of these special times, when the thoughts and feelings of all are in remarkable unison. In such circumstances the Spirit of God can remove many barriers between people and make them realize the essential ties that bind them together: the ties of faith in God. In the midst of an indifferent or unbelieving world they thus bear witness together to God and to humanity.

II
PATHS AND WAYS[2]

As the preceding rapid description of the places and times of dialogue has underscored, dialogue only takes place between people and communities, not between systems of thought or religions. When doctrines or experiences are factors in dialogue it is always as they are lived and expressed by people, themselves involved in a constant process of personal spiritual growth. For this reason true dialogue requires more than a mere knowledge about other people, even if that knowledge includes perfect mastery of their language and culture as well as a full comprehension of their religious tradition. It is necessary that people encounter each other with a willingness to accept each other in mutual understanding, to live alongside each other, to share, to venture and to run risks together.

1. Accepting Each Other

It is time to put an end to an unhappy past of opposition and misunderstanding by following the example of Abraham, who was able to receive his guests at the oaks of Mamre, share the best he had with them, learn from them what would happen to his family and discuss with them the future of the human community. To welcome others in the spirit of Abraham, the "friend of God," is more than just a basic sign of politeness or a rite of traditional courtesy. It involves recognition of and respect for others as they are, even in their difference. Hospitality understood thus can never be satisfied with a merely ephemeral kindness. Receiving others decisively into one's experience and taking their distinctive nature into account provide an opportunity for self-renewal and enrichment.

To accept one another assumes then that Christians and Muslims recognize each other's profound differences, respect each other in the diversity of their religious traditions and try, in meeting, to find out more about each other. This leads to a growth in mutual esteem and love. Every dialogue must begin that way. In the name of truth and realism, we must take full account of the specific religious background of our dialogue partners, with all that it involves of intellectual and emotional attachment. If the absolute good faith and good will of each party are affirmed at the outset, it does not matter if on one side or the other, some are a little too quick to assert that they have the truth or that they are in the right. We should never entertain suspicions that the others are trying stealthily to proselytize us or to impose their kind of dialogue upon us. On the contrary, we should entertain positive expectations for the dialogue and be careful to be fully ready for what it might entail. In that way the Muslim is not just an object to the Christian, nor is the Christian only a curiosity to the Muslim. Finally, believers come to recognize each other fully as persons capable of mutual understanding, and opt to clarify their respective positions, thus going beyond the misunderstanding and prejudices that have accumulated on both sides throughout history.

2. Mutual Understanding

Christians and Muslims are often ignorant of the true identity of one another, even when they think that they possess some knowledge of the other religion. The first need is for objective information on both sides concerning all levels of human spiritual experience. This information should not, however, be solely that of a sociologist or of an Islamist or of a specialist in Christian studies. It must come through mutual acceptance of each other for the discovery not only of who they really are, but also of what they would like to become. Christians owe it to themselves to investigate the Islamic culture, theology and mystical teachings, even as Muslims should learn from Christians the content of their culture, how their theology has developed and what disclosures their mystics have made. By thus informing one another the interlocutors can enter into one another's spiritual resources and gain insight into how they apply them to their personal spiritual journey.

Still, reciprocal information is never enough to make full mutual understanding possible. The interlocutors must rid themselves of all inferiority or superiority complexes, and become ever more receptive of the way those from the other religion explain themselves and their tradition. Gradually, from each side, they should be able to put themselves in the place of the others. It would be ideal if Muslims would finally be capable of presenting Christianity in such a way that Christians would recognize themselves completely, and if Christians could also give a picture of Islam in which Muslims would recognize themselves perfectly.

3. Life Alongside Each Other and Sharing

Called to recognize one another in their authenticity and to give reciprocal witness to their faithfulness, Christians and Muslims need to adapt to each other, to devise ways of favoring unity and to work together wherever they feel mutually motivated by the same values. We cannot stress too much the enormous value of dialogue in circumstances where we eat together, work side by side, endure as in one body the same suffering and enjoy times of celebration with shared pleasure. Through this daily joint experience of the most humble but significant aspects of life Christians and Muslims can help each other to deal with the great questions of the world, humanity and God, even as these were formulated at the end of Chapter One.

So it is perhaps in this way that believers can improve the quality of their life, articulating their hopes for their fellow humans and their aspiration for God. In a relationship of mutuality they must constantly be strong enough to call their own lives into question and to show genuine concern for others. A large part of this concern, to be manifested by both parties, is to make sure that the others are required less and less to suffer the humiliation of being poorly known, poorly understood and poorly received. When we recognize in our partners and in their community all of their excellence as well as their particular virtues, then our dialogue has a good chance of success.

4. To Venture and to Run Risks Together

Any way we look at it, dialogue is an adventure in which the participants are not sure how things will turn out. They are content merely to have confidence in each other, to begin talking and to take action together. They need a certain range of freedom which will permit each party to experiment, taking into full account, of course, the other party and its community. New relationships are thus formed, and whatever their depth or significance at the beginning, they are bound to evolve, grow and bear fruit. Dialogue, involving as it does the free interplay of human initiatives, carries with it a dynamism that even its most severe critics are obliged to recognize.

Whether they like it or not each party in dialogue is revealed to the other. This may cause initial disillusion, and a sense of failure breaking off the interchange. Everyone should be aware of this as a risk to be taken. Dialogue cannot be perfect at its beginning. It is even good to experience times of suspicion and of frustration which will oblige the interlocutors further to clarify to themselves the reasons for their encounter and the motives of their cooperation. It is a very demanding experience to be called to account by those from another religion and to be esteemed by them in terms of what we aspire to be or of what they expect from us. This requires a severe pursuit of truth and a true love for people, along with a faith that has been tested and a generous measure of spiritual wisdom.

III
CHRISTIANS AND THE FAITH OF OTHERS[3]

It is in this spirit of acceptance, understanding and sharing that Christians are called upon by the Church to ponder the mystery of the religious quest as expressed and made concrete by the great historic religions either close at hand or far away. According to the Second Vatican Council, "It [the Council] can provide no more eloquent proof of its solidarity with the entire human family with which it is bound up . . . than by engaging with it in conversation about these various problems which trouble it" (*Gaudium et Spes,* No. 31). "We also turn our thoughts to all who acknowledge God, and who preserve in their traditions precious elements of religion and humanity. We want frank conversation to compel us all to receive the inspirations of the Spirit faithfully and to measure up to them energetically" (*Gaudium et Spes,* No. 92.4). This is why Christians are to "be educated in the ecumenical spirit, and duly prepared for fraternal dialogue with non-Christians" (*Ad Gentes,* No. 16).

Above all Christians should respect the personal faith and religious tradition of others, "gladly and reverently laying bare the seeds of the Word which lie hidden in them" (*Ad Gentes,* No. 11), and which bear witness to the work of the Holy Spirit (*Ad Gentes,* No. 15). In fact the "multiple endeavors, including religious ones, by which men search for God," even if they "need to be enlightened and purified," can sometimes "serve as a guidance course toward the true God, or as a preparation for the gospel" (*Ad Gentes,* No. 3; *Lumen Gentium,* No. 16). Thus dialogue is presented by the Council as the means, both human and Christian, for bringing the attitude of spiritual hospitality to its fullest development: "sincere and patient dialogue" (*Ad Gentes,* No. 11); "mutual esteem, reverence, and harmony . . . with ever abounding fruitfulness" (*Gaudium et Spes,* No. 92).

When we meditate on the mystery of salvation in the spirit of the

Council, we see how strikingly salvation is linked with the coming of the Kingdom of God among humankind. This is precisely what took place long ago when Jesus Christ came to Palestine. Now this universal spiritual Kingdom of peace, justice and forgiveness can never be identified with any concrete reality, lest it be thus limited in its scope. And, since it is a living Kingdom, its growth passes through the same phases as the paschal mystery of suffering, death and resurrection, whose universal and eternal fecundity was revealed by Jesus Christ. It is the responsibility of Christians, united in the Church, to witness that all humanity is called upon to enter that Kingdom, and to labor by all means to that end. No human activity and no religious dialogue are alien to the Kingdom of God. Faith is nourished and its expression renewed by the encounter with other cultures, both secular and religious, past or present. Nothing falls outside the all-embracing reach of the Spirit of God. For Christians dialogue as we have described it is in no sense foreign to the full manifestation of the mystery of Christ, who is the alpha and omega of history.

When Christians reread the history of their faith as it is given in the Bible, they are struck by the fact that, according to that history, when a people are chosen by God it is for the blessing of all humanity. In fact the covenant with Abraham (renewed later with Moses) is situated within the universal covenant with Noah. And this latter is only the renewal of the covenant that was made at the time of creation between God and humanity. So the Abrahamic covenant was made for the benefit of all peoples, and the great prophets of Israel recalled this truth many times when a narrow spirit of religious nationalism wanted to appropriate it too much for itself. Does not history record how the "nations" played a part in "salvation history"? Jesus Christ Himself showed all during His life His respect for the faith and devotion of others, by proclaiming that no one is excluded from the Kingdom of God, be they sinners or righteous, Samaritans or Galileans, a Roman centurion or a Judean Pharisee. All can enter the one Kingdom of God when they turn to the Lord in conversion and lead thereafter a new life of love for God and for others.

In faithfulness to this summons to the Kingdom of God, and in conformity to the spirit of the Second Vatican Council, Christians can discover, as they reflect theologically on non-Christian religions, a new impulsion to respect, esteem and dialogue, under the guidance of the Spirit of God. For too long Christian theology was only preoccupied with the "salvation of the unbelievers," without asking itself about the ultimate significance of the other religions. Finally the theologians have begun to consider what might be the specific mission of those religions. The Council aptly reminded us that the Church should not venture into such an investigation without having well-defined ideas concerning salvation,

Jesus Christ, the Church and faith. Theologians have always admitted that a non-Christian of good faith can be saved, but they have differed greatly as concerns the modalities of that salvation. Generally it is affirmed that the faith which saves consists of life commitment to an absolute. That option is confirmed and its seriousness before God guaranteed by the evidence of a pure conscience and a moral life.

Christians who seek to follow the example of the early Church in their encounter with people who are different from themselves will realize that the New Testament speaks of several different attitudes toward non-Christians. Which one is adopted will depend on the particular circumstances, or upon the spiritual affinity felt toward one or another attitude. It is possible to adopt first one position and then another, or even to feel two motivations simultaneously. There is first of all the joyous proclamation of the way of salvation in Jesus Christ, as practiced by Peter and Paul in the Acts of the Apostles (Acts 2:38; I Corinthians 1:17), and which represents the basic Christian missionary duty. Then there is also the witness of Christians of the "dispersion" to whom Peter says, "Maintain good conduct among the Gentiles, so that . . . they may see your good deeds and glorify God on the day of visitation" (I Peter 2:12). Even as Christ is the "witness of the Father," Christians, in turn, are called to be "witnesses of Jesus Christ." This is brought out clearly in the Gospel and Epistles of John. Sometimes Christians can, in various situations, even share the feelings of Paul who, when faced with intransigent non-Christian brothers and sisters, wrote of his "sadness" and his "anguish," but at the same time observed "that they have a zeal for God" (Romans 10:2). He was convinced that God would not reject them (Romans 11:1). Through such a variety of possible attitudes, and faced with the insoluble mystery of religious plurality, respect, understanding and esteem are necessary qualities for the Christian, because "of its very nature, the exercise of religion consists before all else in those internal, voluntary, and free acts whereby man sets the course of his life directly toward God. No merely human power can either command or prohibit acts of this kind" (*Dignitatis Humanae,* No. 3).

IV
BELIEVERS IN DIALOGUE

Besides the human desire to be mutually accepted, to understand one another, to lead lives of sharing, and also the will to venture and run risks together, Christians and Muslims are led by their particular motivations to consider the specifically religious dimensions of the dialogue. Faced with persons of another faith Christians must ponder the history of salvation, as they know it, together with the significance of the other great historic religions and the forms of devotion through which the Spirit of God is manifested in a multitude of unexpected ways. And Muslims, in their turn, can find Christians to be very special interlocutors, as "People of Scripture," to whom God has sent prophets and whom He expects to submit to Him in obedient gratitude.

1. Dialogue in God's Presence and in Dependence Upon Him

Both Muslims and Christians have the conviction that human beings are not the result of chance or of determinism, but that they are part of a marvelous plan of the living and eternal God, who wills finally to bring together into community all whom He has created. Sharing this conviction they feel constrained to commit themselves unreservedly in good faith to the venture of dialogue. Christians know, for their part, that they have been created "in the image of God" (Genesis 1:27) in order to become "partakers of the divine nature" (II Peter 1:4) and "be called children of God" (I John 3:1) by virtue of a wondrous identification with the Word incarnate, Jesus Christ. In turn, Muslims believe that they have been harmoniously fashioned by God and made responsible for a "mission" (*amana*) which "the heavens and the earth and the hills . . . shrank from bearing" (Qur'an 33:72). In view of this exalted vision seen from the two vantage points of faith the dialogue of Muslims and Christians cannot avoid involvement with the creative design and providential action of the One who probes their conscience, brings them together and teaches them what to say and do. In truth God is present with each person, "nearer to him than his jugular vein" (Qur'an 50:16), so that in dialogue the participants can say with the Psalmist, "O Lord, thou has searched me and known me . . . thou discernest my thoughts from afar . . . and art acquainted with all my ways. Even before a word is on my tongue, lo, O Lord, thou knowest it altogether. Thou dost beset me behind and before, and layest thy hand upon me" (Psalm 139:1–5).

So at whatever level their exchanges may take place, Christians and Muslims acknowledge that they are witnesses for God, supremely concerned to serve Him and to gain His good pleasure. They both are attentive to His claims upon them, realizing that the closer they draw near to one another, the more aware they become of His presence with them. Even though they differ greatly in both the content and the expression of their faith, Muslims and Christians are aware of their common concern to bear witness to the presence of God and to live in deeper awareness of that presence by faith and hope. Meeting, even for a limited time, "in the name of God" should give them both the conviction that in such encounter their dignity and reciprocal enrichment are set forth. Is not God Himself the source of all that is authentic and holy in the faithful witness of those who stand in continuity with their fathers, brothers and sisters in the same faith?

When Muslims and Christians are willing to accept each other as true "witnesses of God" and "servants of His word," they can better help one another to be submissive to His Spirit of guidance and inspiration. Dialogue between believers in faith can only be the work of God's Spirit, even if they have different, even contrasting views on the identity and action of that Spirit. Christians know, for their part, that the Spirit is that advocate and counselor of believers who comes to "convince the world of sin and of righteousness and of judgment" (John 16:8), and to "guide you into all the truth" (John 16:13). It is this openness to divine judgment that moves believers, when engaged in dialogue, to seek clarity, gentleness, confidence and prudence in all of their activities together. And the atmosphere of dialogue impels them respectively ever to "enlarge the place of the tent," in openness to those of the other faith, who strive to be true to its demands.

2. Conversion to God and Reconciliation with One Another

In loyalty, believers must be both consistent with their own faith and at one with the community which has conveyed that faith to them, nourishing them in its tradition of devotion. They must see concordance between the normative expression of religion and their personal experience. If Christians and Muslims are mutually to strive toward greater faithfulness and a more vital influence upon one another, then they must be fully aware both of the things which unite them and the things which divide them. Nothing would be more detrimental to true dialogue than a false effort at accommodation whereby Christians, for example, would seek to make their faith acceptable to Muslims. Dialogue would lose its meaning if Christian participants reduced their faith to generalities and toned down the doctrines which diverge from statements in the Qur'an. In dialogue Muslims must encounter Christians in the fullness of their spiritual life and the integrity of Christian doctrine. In the same way Christians must come to understand and appreciate Muslims in the wholeness of their way of worship and in the fullness of their belief system. This is a fundamental requirement of truth and loyalty in which the honor of God Himself is at stake.

The foregoing makes clear that believers engaged in dialogue are already in a position of greater faithfulness toward their common Lord and enjoy a deeper grasp of truth than was the case before their dialogue began. To be where they are in mutual encounter presupposes a difficult spiritual development, whereby they have given up prejudices, opened their hearts to others, and, in general, abandoned previous ideas and attitudes which were hindrances to the full flowering of their faith. In a word, they have rededicated themselves to God, in defiance of the spiritual "idols" which abound, ancient and modern politics conducted "in the name of God," exclusive ideologies, self-satisfied pharisaisms, etc.

Conversion to God, as described above, is the only thing that can give us true spiritual freedom. It is not a question of changing from one religion to another under the influence of various sociological and ideological factors. Believers reject such proselytism unanimously as unworthy of the faith by which they live and the God whom they serve. On the contrary, true dialogue presupposes a "spiritual conversion" in which sin is recognized and God's forgiveness is sought for the wrong of failing to appreciate the religious experience of others. By His pardon God alone can purify our faith and transform our hearts. Out of that experience will come new awareness of the demands of justice and love, thus making possible a greater degree of mutual respect and friendship.

3. Holding One Another to the Highest Ideals of Witness

When Christians and Muslims realize that first of all God is witness to their dialogue and that conversion to Him is its first requirement, they are able to develop their exchanges in a spirit of humility and truth. They proceed in an atmosphere of reconciliation, unconcerned about winning a victory over one another or bringing the other over to one's own position, or, even less, engaging in a formal round of niceties or show of amiability. Dialogue is mutual challenge from the standpoint of faith and fraternal emulation in action, carried out "in the name of God." It shows "enduring patience (avoiding) polemics and compromise . . . in alert openness toward others, constantly seeking to assimilate the deep values of faith, all in the atmosphere of clear witness."[4]

In dialogue thus understood, Christians and Muslims are for one another "reminders" and "monitors." By the example of Muslims, Christians are called back to the spiritual responsibilities of being children of God in Jesus Christ, of an all-embracing love which demands the dedication of self. The Islamic confession of faith, the communal witness of ritual prayer, almsgiving, fasting and pilgrimage are all seen as authentic religious values. Believers cannot be unmoved by the workings of faith in the personal and communal life of others. They see there a call by the Spirit of God to be better witnesses for God and more faithful servants of His Word. Are not the fruits of the Spirit called: "love, joy, peace, patience, kindness, goodness, faithfulness, gentleness, self-control" (Galatians 5:22–23)?

When Christians and Muslims dialogue in such an atmosphere they are able to grow toward the fullness which they believe to be the divine intent, constantly sounding their conscience as to the quality of their faith, the consistency of their behavior and the demands of their personal calling. A Christian will ask: Why am I a Christian? Why has Jesus Christ by His life, death and resurrection, given me eternal life, made me able to call God Father and all human beings brothers and sisters? Believers will need to devise a common language for dialogue after having carefully studied the words and symbols which belong to their respective particularities. Through these necessary stages, as well as the stimulation of mutual example, God will prepare hearts and minds for dialogue at the highest level, that is, in contemplation of the "unfathomable mystery of God's plan and the human condition."

Such is the holy, spiritual emulation to which Christians and Muslims are called in dialogue. The latter know, from the Qur'an, that "had Allah willed He could have made you one community. But that He may try you by that which He hath given you (He hath made you as ye are). So vie one with another in good works. Unto Allah ye will all return" (Qur'an 5:48). As for the Christians, they can take inspiration from these words of Saint Paul: "Brethren, whatever is true, whatever is honorable, whatever is just, whatever is pure, whatever is lovely, whatever is gracious, if there is any excellence, if there is anything worthy of praise, think about these things" (Philippians 4:8). They remember that modesty is enjoined on them: "I bid every one among you not to think of himself more highly than he ought to think, but to think with sober judgment, each according to the measure of faith which God has assigned him" (Romans 12:3). So Muslims and Christians should seek to excel each other in good deeds of faith such as the promotion of life, justice and peace, the defense of human rights, in all of which they acknowledge the greatness of God, giving Him the honor which is His due.

4. Undertake the Impossible, but Accept the Provisional

It is also a fact that dialogue is a risky venture, especially if the partners mean to go beyond its initial stages of acceptance and listening to one another. However, the hope which believers have in the power of God to bring humans together in unity inspires them to undertake anything that has this final goal in view, even if it is impossible according to conventional wisdom and prudence.

It is also true that the meeting of a Muslim and a Christian to the degree of human and religious intensity which has been described above carries with it a certain sense of contradiction. Each of the two religions, Islam and Christianity, considers itself to be universal in its overall plan of salvation. Christians believe that every person on earth is called to know God the Father through the mysterious and marvelous configuration of the Word Incarnate, Jesus Christ. Muslims have the conviction that every person on earth is intended to live in complete submission to God according to the faith of Islam. Does one or the other party lack in honesty or sincerity if they try to carry on dialogue to the demanding degree described above, while all the time they have such convictions in their hearts about the universality of their message? Of course not, especially if they believe that God Most High is sovereign even over the diversity of their respective communities, and that He will someday, in His good time, let them know why "they differed." Until that time each group must confess that, if they did not desire for the others that which they deem most precious, then they would be falling short of the full acceptance and sharing which were set forth in the preceding discussion of religious dialogue. The most precious thing to believers is precisely their own faith and the degree of access which it grants to the more or less inaccessible plenitude of God.

Should Muslims be forbidden the desire to see their Christian friends become Muslims, or, similarly, do Christians not have the right to wish that their Muslim friends become Christians? They should not be denied such a desire, for otherwise there would be an undue limitation to their desire for sharing with others. Muslims will know that a famous hadith says, "No one is truly a believer who does not love for others that which he loves for himself."[5] Christians have heard from Jesus himself as a commandment that is ancient, but also ever new: "You shall love your neighbor as yourself" (Matthew 22:39), "Love one another even as I have loved you . . ." (John 13:34). So there is no reason why Christians and Muslims should not wish that they should meet someday in the same faith, and in identical worship, whenever God wills it, and however He wills it. Such desires are legitimate even if practically speaking they effectively exclude each other. This is what is meant by undertaking the impossible. And yet it should be ventured, in the name of God: to practice mutual acceptance to the limit and then acknowledge that full concurrence is as yet unachievable. Such is the inherent contradiction in dialogue when it is seriously pursued.

It is important to mention here a subtle danger that threatens the practice of dialogue. This is the suspicion, well founded or not, that one's partners in the exchanges have ulterior motives of proselytism. Some people even criticize dialogue as being a new method, even a skillful maneuver, to bring the partner over to the ideology or to the faith of the one who has taken the initiative. It must be repeated again that true dialogue presupposes that the participants have no intention of changing the other's religion nor even of instilling doubts regarding the faith of the others. Such intentions would be a parody or a betrayal of authentic dialogue, which is intended to progress under the eye of God and by the action of His Spirit. Rather the partners should seek to help each other toward an ever-deepening personal conversion to God and a fuller obedience to Him.

Realizing that dialogue depends first of all on the will and wisdom of God, and that He is faithful to His promises, believers found their enterprise on hope, making do with the provisional state of things, even if it is unsatisfactory. In that way they witness that their dialogue transcends them and that their hope lends an element of surprise to their exchanges. Somewhat like travelers, they do not know exactly where God is leading them, but they recognize that He wants them to go along together, even if they are different. He alone knows about the outcome of the dialogue, and in His wisdom He reminds believers that their situation is always provisional, that they have to devise new forms of dialogue, as inspired by His Spirit, depending on the immediate circumstances of the encounter. Courage is demanded of Muslims and Christians to accept an impossible duty, whose accomplishment depends upon the One for whom nothing is impossible.

Those who are courageous enough to take part in dialogue will want to ponder what lies beyond such activity, that is, what will happen to those who follow the leading of God in mutual encounter. Since they belong to religions having universal scope they must recognize the importance of the missionary imperative in each tradition. Each community has the duty to offer its treasure of faith, obedience and love to others, inviting them to share the gifts received from God. Of course such an intent presupposes and requires complete respect for the choice made by any person of a particular religious tradition, even if such choice involves a change of religion in order better to respond to what the conscience feels to be the call of God.

The Second Vatican Council issued a timely reminder to Christians of the modern understanding of "religious freedom," which "has its foundation in the very dignity of the human person, as this dignity is known through the revealed Word of God and by reason itself" (*Dignitatis humanae*, No. 2), so that "no one is to be forced to embrace the Christian faith against his own will" (*Dignitatis humanae*, No. 10). Coming as one result, perhaps, of dialogue, and also transcending it, is the free personal choice of religious faith, evoked by the image of Abraham in his exemplary and humble submission to the mysterious decrees of God.

There is another experience that transcends dialogue. It is shared by Christians and Muslims who are willing to pay the price of true encounter, and consists of the joyful recognition that they are much closer to each other than they had thought. This sense of closeness increases as they progress together in service and in the confidence of faith. The will of a Holy God to unite all humanity cannot fail to bring Muslims and Christians together more and more, as they daily witness the signs of holiness in the lives of one another. They come to realize that they love each other "in God" (*mutahabbuna fi-Allah*), and they show forth the consequences of that love in the societies of which they are a part. At this stage the Christian, at least, can say with Jesus Christ, "Whoever does the will of God is my brother, and sister, and mother" (Mark 3:35).

Notes

1. Besides the titles given in the Bibliography, see *Islamochristiana* for a description of certain local situations of dialogue: Michael L. Fitzgerald, "Christian-Muslim Dialogue in South-East Asia," in No. 2 (1976), pp. 171–185; Ali Merad, "Rapports de l'Eglise avec les Musulmans d'Europe," in No. 3 (1977), pp. 197–205; Michel Lelong, "Le Secrétariat de l'Eglise de France pour les Relations avec l'Islam," in No. 4 (1978), pp. 165–174; Christian W. Troll, "Christian-Muslim Relations in India, A Critical Survey," in No. 5 (1979), pp. 119–145; Michel Lagarde, "Quelques aspects concrets du dialogue islamo-chrétien au Mali," in No. 5 (1979), pp. 147–170; Joseph Kenny, "Christian-Muslim Relations in Nigeria," in No. 5 (1979), pp. 171–192; Penelope Johnstone, "Christians and Muslims in Britain," in No. 7 (1981), pp. 167–199 and in No. 12 (1986), pp. 181–190; Marston Speight, "Christian-Muslim Dialogue in the United States of America," in No. 7 (1981), pp. 201–210; Peter G. Gowing, "Christian-Muslim Dialogue in the Philippines, 1976–1981," in No. 7 (1981), pp. 211–225; Laurence P. Fitzgerald, "Christians and Muslims in Australia," in No. 10 (1984), pp. 159–176; Gerrie Lubbe, "Muslims and Christians in South Africa," in No. 13 (1987), pp. 113–129; Achilles de Souza, "Dialogue in the Islamic Republic of Pakistan," in No. 14 (1988), pp. 211–218; Piet Reesink, "Chrétiens et Musulmans au Pays Bas," in No. 14 (1988), pp. 237–253; Heinze Klautke, "Muslim and Christian Relations in West Germany," in No. 14 (1988), pp. 255–266.

2. Besides the titles given in the Bibliography, see *Islamochristiana* for the following studies: Ali Merad, "Dialogue islamo-chrétien: pour la recherche d'un langage commun," in No. 1 (1975), pp. 1–10; Roger Arnaldez, "Dialogue islamo-chrétien et sensibilités religieuses," in No. 1 (1975), pp. 11–23; Mohammad Talbi, "Islam et dialogue (Réflexions sur un thème d'actualité)," in Arabic, in No. 4 (1978), pp. 1–26 (the French text was published in Tunis, in 1972, and reedited in 1979 by the Maison Tunisiènne de l'Edition, 51 pp.); Mo-

44   *Dialogue between Christians and Muslims*

hammad Talbi, "Une communauté de communautés (Le droit à la différence et les voies de l'harmonie), in No. 4 (1978), pp. 11–25; David A. Kerr, "Christian Witness in Relation to Muslim Neighbors," in No. 10 (1984), pp. 1–30.

3. See especially in *Islamochristiana,* Louis Gardet, "La foi du Chrétien et les grandes cultures religieuses," in No. 3 (1977), pp. 11–38; Joseph Gelot, "Vers une théologie chrétienne des religions non chrétiennes" (with a full bibliography), in No. 2 (1976), pp. 1–57; and Claude Geffré, La théologie des religions non chrétiennes vingt ans après Vatican II," in No. 11 (1985), pp. 115–133. See also Secretariat for Non-Christians, *The Attitude of the Church towards the Followers of Other Religions,* 1984.

4. Mohammed Talbi, *Islam et dialogue . . .* (French text), p. 23.

5. The thirteenth of the forty-two *hadiths* found, with commentary in the classical work, *The Forty Hadith,* by Al-Nawawi (1233–77). The author comments: "it is preferable to understand this as referring to all people, unbelievers as well as Muslims. The latter desire for their unbelieving friends that which they desire for themselves, that is, that they should become Muslims, and for their fellow Muslims that they should persevere in the faith of Islam."

Chapter Three
Recognizing the Values of Others

When Christians become aware of the extreme variety of Muslim life and expression in the world, and as they seek better ways of dialogue with Muslims, it is only natural for them to give attention to the authentic values of faith and life in the communities of Islam. This subject should be approached with a sense of intellectual fairness as well as a charitable spirit. Books can give scholarly insight, but they will never take the place of direct contact with members of different Muslim communities.

The ideals of faith and everyday practices are not necessarily the same. To be just in dialogue the partners must clearly distinguish between the two. In all honesty and loyalty we must recognize that every practice by believers is an attempt, however incomplete it may be, to exemplify the ideals of their faith. It is more just for partners in dialogue to compare their respective practices and then to investigate together the ideals which lie behind those practices. Since these pages are addressed first of all to Christians, it is normal that the essential points of Muslims' faith here presented should be those which will evoke the most immediate respect and which Christians will most easily be able to interpret according to the spirit of their own faith.

I
SUBMISSION TO GOD[1]

The Islamic ideal is to live in complete submission to God (*islam*), both individually and collectively. Muslims reflect the spirit of original monotheism as it was revealed by God to Adam, the first prophet, and then to Abraham, "the friend of God," the first "submissive one" (*muslim*) in history (Qur'an 3:67), and subsequently reflected through the ages by all true believers. According to Islam the original Abrahamic monotheism was changed or distorted by Jews and Christians, and then restored to its original purity and simplicity by the Qur'an which Muhammad, the prophet of Islam, conveyed to all humanity. This monotheistic faith is that which belongs to "human nature as created by God" (*fitra*), the faith practiced by the *hanifs* and offered to all human beings as the model of perfect religion. "Lo! religion with Allah (is) The Surrender (to His will and guidance) (*islam*)" (Qur'an 3:19). In fact, God "hath ordained for you that religion which He commended unto Noah, and that which We commended unto Abraham and Moses and Jesus, saying: Establish the religion, and be not divided therein" (Qur'an 42:13).

In the view of Muslims Islam is not a new religion. It simply reestablishes true monotheism, restoring humankind to the place of faithfulness toward God, thus fulfilling, from the human side, the primordial "covenant of allegiance" (*mithaq*) which was made with the Creator. "And (remember) when thy Lord brought forth from the Children of Adam, from their reins, their seed, and made them testify of themselves (saying): Am I not your Lord? They said: Yea, verily. We testify" (Qur'an 7:172).

A believer's dignity is found in complete submission to the universal lordship of God, with all that such an attitude involves of surrender, confidence and obedience. Submission means an active attachment to the will of God and a voluntary, tranquil and deliberate committal of oneself to the infinite divine wisdom.

The state of mind corresponding to this spiritual commitment is a constant dependence upon God (*tawakkul*). Believers entrust their future, their concerns and their possessions to Him who is the best of guardians, for "Allah is sufficient as Trustee" (Qur'an 4:81) and "Most Excellent is He in Whom we trust" (Qur'an 3:173). They affirm in truth, "My welfare is only in Allah. In Him I trust and unto Him I turn (repentant)" (Qur'an 11:88). One of the ninety-nine Beautiful Names of God also refers to the security which is guaranteed to believers. God is the one who ensures the security (*mu'min*) of the believer (*mu'min*), who thus finds safety in God. This is the meaning of the act of believing, or faith (*iman*).

Certainly this spirit of submission does not mean for Muslims that they avoid their responsibilities or show an attitude of resignation. It rather enables them to avoid the temptations of pride and presumption which all people confront in their inner beings. By choosing to call themselves by the title, "servant of God" (*'abd Allah*), they do not deny their freedom as human beings, but rather affirm that everything comes from God and returns to Him, and that human beings can in no way claim to be His partners or associates. Both reformers and modernists within the Muslim community insist that "submission" (*islam*) constitutes the dignity, grandeur and responsibility of believers, while at the same time affirming that God is the source of it as well as its goal. Submission is, then, an active and responsible attachment to the will of God.

At the same time this *islam* of body and soul enables Muslims to show an admirable spirit of patient endurance in times of trial and suffering, and in the hour of death, since "Allah is with the steadfast" (Qur'an 2:153). Christians can appreciate and respect this religious attitude of Muslims, remembering that it also characterized Abraham and the great prophets of history, and especially Jesus, son of Mary, who was led to accept the suffering and death of the cross. As Christians exemplify this attitude themselves, in union with Jesus Christ, they will be able better to understand and esteem their Muslim associates. They will perceive that Islam provides three important means to help adherents of that faith to accomplish their submission (*islam*): meditation on a book, the imitation of a prophet and the support of a community.

II
MEDITATION ON A BOOK[2]

Muslims consider the Qur'an to be the divine message transmitted directly to Muhammad in "clear Arabic speech" (Qur'an 16:103), in the course of his preaching in Mecca and Medina. The chapters, or *suras*, are classified as Meccan or Medinan, but in the book they are arranged, not in chronological order, but according to their decreasing length. The 114 suras, with their evocative titles, contain 6,236 verses, which make the Qur'an a book about the size of the New Testament. To Muslims the holy book constitutes the final, definitive and perfect revelation of previous books (Torah, or Pentateuch, Psalms and Gospel), which were only the first and uncompleted versions of a text containing the very words of God taken from the eternally existent "Well-guarded Tablet."

Since it was directly revealed by God and sent down to earth in progressive sequences, the Qur'an possesses the uncreated character of the eternal Word, at least in its content, if not in its manner of formulation. The classical interpretation is that the holy book is not simply inspired, for God alone is its author and the Prophet Muhammad merely transmitted it, without inserting any of himself into it. This is why it is called an abiding miracle (*mu'jiza*), forever inimitable. "Say: Verily, though mankind and Jinn should assemble to produce the like of this Qur'an, they could not produce the like thereof though they were helpers one of another" (Qur'an 17:88). By virtue of the great beauty of its literary form and its sounds, the book gratifies the esthetic sense of Muslims. It also satisfies their need to meditate upon the signs which speak of God, of humankind and of the world. As they see in it the eternal Word of God made accessible to humanity in time, one can say that the Qur'an has for them a function somewhat similar to that of Jesus Christ in Christianity. In Islam the Qur'an is the Word of God made scripture.

The Qur'an constitutes the primary nourishment for the faith of Muslims, as they learn it by heart in childhood and have it constantly brought to mind through the many channels of Arab-Islamic culture. The holy Scripture is also one of the main foundations of Arab civilization. It was in order to understand the text better that Arab Muslims developed their sciences of grammar and lexicography and pursued their research in philosophy and theology. They applied to these disciplines such a wealth of intellectual effort and produced results full of such profound wisdom that all meditation upon the Qur'an which is in continuity with the past is enriched immeasurably. The holy text provides the essential element of Islamic liturgy, and its message is constantly set forth, both by the learned and by the unlettered of the community of faith.

Christians observe how deeply meditation on the Qur'an penetrates the life of their Muslim associates, for the latter have been saying together for fourteen centuries: "This is the Scripture wherein there is no doubt, a guidance unto those who ward off (evil): who believe in the unseen . . . and who believe in that which is revealed unto thee (Muhammad) and that which was revealed before thee, and are certain of the Hereafter" (Qur'an 2:2–4). Christians also recognize in the Qur'an parts of their biblical heritage, that which they already share with their Jewish brothers and sisters. Many passages remind them of Psalms of creation, certain prophetic texts or wisdom verses from Proverbs or Ecclesiastes. Others seem to be reproducing or interpreting certain legal chapters from Leviticus or traditions from the apocryphal Gospels.

Thus the content of the Qur'an is quite analogous to that of the Bible, especially the Old Testament. Regardless of some decisive differences between the two texts, including some outright denials in the Qur'an of important biblical affirmations, the Muslim Scripture shares in the content of the biblical message as contained in the Old Testament and even in the New Testament. When Muslims seek to meditate on the text constantly, to apply it and practice it in their personal and communal lives, they are manifesting religious attitudes which are common to Jews and Christians. Because these last have for so long maintained the same attitudes and practices with reference to their Scriptures, they should be able to appreciate the parallel orientation of their Muslim associates.

As Christians learn the content of the Qur'an they will be able to speak about it with respect, pointing out all that seems to correspond with the biblical message and calling attention clearly and tactfully to that which seems to differ from the Christian Scriptures. They will realize that when Muslims talk about the text of their Scripture they say, "God Most High said . . ." and to avoid offense Christians will not use expressions such as, ". . . as Muhammad says in the Qur'an." Muslims do not expect that Christians will hold to the conviction of Islam, so they will be content if the latter say, "The Qur'an declares that . . ." or "It is written in the Qur'an. . . ." Such expressions show respect for both Christian and Muslim feelings. Of course, for Christians divine revelation culminates in Jesus Christ, the Word made flesh, and every book which speaks of God must be appreciated in terms of that regulating principle, and according to the rules of sound religious judgment regarding "inspired books." Does this mean that it is possible or even advisable to develop a "Christian reading" of the Qur'an that would have little relationship with the Muslim experience of fourteen centuries? If Christians should venture to undertake such an enterprise, they would certainly have no right to impose its methods and conclusions upon their Muslim friends. By the same token it would be inappropriate for Muslims to impose upon Christians a "Muslim reading" of the Gospels.

III
THE IMITATION OF A PROPHETIC MODEL

Thanks to the Qur'an and to Muhammad who transmitted it to them, Muslims have the possibility of knowing certain biblical prophets, of being attracted by their message and captivated by their example. In fact one of the most important functions of the Qur'anic message was to remind believers, as it did to Meccan polytheists of old, that God never abandons a people, but that He is concerned to send messengers to all, "as bearers of good news and warners" (Qur'an 6:48). He communicated to Muhammad that "We have sent already unto peoples that were before thee, and We visited them with tribulation and adversity" (Qur'an 6:42) because they did not accept the message nor did they humble themselves before God to obey His laws.

So, Muslims are called to ponder the unity and continuity of the message of the prophets throughout what might be called an Islamic "sacred history." The Qur'an presents the essence of that message as being the strict monotheism of the beginnings and the abiding necessity for human beings to worship the one God, to submit to His law and to follow His "prophet" (*nabi*) or His "messenger" (*rasul*). According to this view, the religion of God is one and the same, even though it is revealed repeatedly to different peoples in their particular languages. Those privileged witnesses who bear the message are the divinely chosen prophets. They are sent to rebellious peoples and experience suspicion, mockery and persecution. Only a small number accept their message, while the masses who have heard the divine call but have rejected it finally endure a terrible punishment. Then at the end of their careers the prophets enjoy divine vindication and victory.

Who are these prophetic witnesses whose lives, revelatory words and final victory are recounted by the Qur'an? Their names can nearly all be found in the Bible, although Jews and Christians note the absence of Isaiah, Jeremiah, Ezekiel, Daniel and other prophets after them in the Old Testament. The Qur'anic text affirms, "That is Our argument. We gave it unto Abraham against his folk. . . . And we bestowed upon him Isaac and Jacob . . . and Noah did We guide aforetime; and of his seed (We guided) David and Solomon and Job and Joseph and Moses and Aaron. . . . And Zachariah and John and Jesus and Elias. . . . And Ishmael and Elisha and Jonah and Lot" (Qur'an 6:83–86). Other verses add to this long list the names of Adam, Dhu al-Kifl (Joshua?), Idris (Enoch?), Hud, Salih and Shu'ayb. All of these prophets do not, however, have the same importance, and the number of verses given to Moses (502), Abraham (245), Noah (131) and Jesus (93) show that these personalities represent the times of the most significant divine intervention in human affairs. Such are the great prophetic models which Muslims are intended to imitate, and upon which they are to meditate, although, of course, the Qur'an is clear in distinguishing Muhammad as "the Seal of the Prophets" (Qur'an 33:40).

1. Abraham[3]

Abraham (Ibrahim), "the friend of God" (*Khalil Allah*), is the great witness of monotheism and the brave destroyer of idols. "He said unto his father: O my father! Why worshippest thou that which heareth not nor seeth, nor can in aught avail thee? O my father! Lo! there hath come unto me of knowledge that which came not unto thee. So follow me, and I will lead thee on a right path" (Qur'an 19:42,43). At another time he said to his opponents, "Dispute ye with me concerning Allah when He hath guided me" (Qur'an 6:80)? "Your Lord is the Lord of the heavens and the earth, Who created them; and I am of those who testify unto that" (Qur'an 21:56). His simple reply to those who contradicted him was "Lo! I am going unto my Lord Who will guide me" (Qur'an 37:99). Such a submissive spirit enabled him to receive the messengers of God who announced to him the destruction of the sinful cities and the birth of Isaac. As the first "submissive one" (*muslim*) of history he was willing to sacrifice even the son whom God had given him, the son whose name the Qur'an strangely does not mention in the passage regarding this event.[4] Finally a "mighty sacrificial victim" was substituted for his son. This act of exemplary obedience is commemorated each year by one of the rites of the pilgrimage to Mecca. This rite, the "great festival" (*al-'id al-kabir*), is also called the "festival of sacrifice" (*'id al-adha*).

In the Medinan suras Abraham appears as the one who restored and purified the Temple (*Ka'ba*) of Mecca with the help of his son, Ishmael, as the prophetic intercessor in favor of the "mother of cities" (Mecca), and as the founder of the true worship of one God, the faith of the hanifs (monotheists). Islam is thus presented as the perfect restoration of Abrahamic monotheism. Christians and Jews find then in this model many of the traits which the Book of Genesis mentions concerning "their father in the faith," and they can rejoice that "the Islamic faith is pleased to associate itself" with the example of Abraham in order to "submit wholeheartedly" to the "inscrutable decrees" of God (*Nostra Aetate,* No. 3). Of course certain important differences exist, since nothing is said about the promises made to Abraham that he would have a land and especially a posterity by which "shall all the nations of the earth bless themselves" (Genesis 22:18). Further, the preference given to Ishmael as opposed to Isaac, and the opposition which results between peoples who are attached to one or the other, raise problems and create conflicts. Nevertheless those who are dedicated to the practice of dialogue should never forget that all of them together have a "goodly pattern . . . in Abraham and those with him" (Qur'an 60:4).

2. Moses

Moses (*Musa*), "with whom God spoke directly" (*Kalim Allah*), is to Muslims quite similar to the figure whom Jews and Christians find in the Book of Exodus. In the Qur'an he says to his family, "I see a fire afar off. . . . Peradventure I may . . . find guidance at the fire" (Qur'an 20:10). And in fact God speaks to him, saying, "I have chosen thee, so hearken unto that which is inspired. Lo! I, even I, am Allah. There is no God save Me. So serve Me and establish worship for My remembrance" (Qur'an 20:13–14). Proofs of this revelation are given. There is his staff which becomes "a serpent, gliding," and his hand which comes forth from under his arm "white without hurt" (Qur'an 20:20–23). Then Moses, accompanied by his brother Aaron, goes "unto Pharaoh," for "Lo! he hath transgressed" (Qur'an 20:24). His first mission seems to have been to try to turn Pharaoh and his people to true monotheism before obtaining from him permission to lead the Children of Israel into the desert.

The time of testing in the desert and the sin of idolatry which his people committed lead Moses to be a messenger of monotheism to them.

This is why he receives the Scripture (Torah) on Mount Sinai and destroys the golden calf which the Children of Israel had built upon the instigation of the "Samaritan" who "misled them" (Qur'an 20:85). After that his people only show ingratitude toward him, in spite of the repeated signs which he is given, such as bringing water out of the rock, and providing manna and quails. So the people are condemned to wander in the desert for forty years. Moses dies alone, abandoned by all, after going through a mysterious experience. The Qur'an points out the high privilege that was given him: "We called him from the right slope of the Mount, and brought him nigh in communion" (Qur'an 19:53). This is perhaps why Moses tried to go beyond his double role of prophet and messenger and ask for more. "And when Moses came to Our appointed tryst and his Lord had spoken unto him, he said: My Lord! Show me (Thy self), that I may gaze upon Thee. He said: Thou wilt not see Me, but gaze upon the mountain! If it stand still in its place, then thou wilt see Me. And when his Lord revealed (His) glory to the mountain He sent it crashing down. And Moses fell down senseless" (Qur'an 7:143).

Such is the second prophetic model which the Qur'an presents to those who meditate upon its text. Its characteristics are similar to those mentioned in the Bible previously. Moses spoke with God, risking a face-to-face encounter with him. The prophet was able to confront Pharaoh and Egyptian power, liberate his people, and transmit the Law to them in the desert. He also tried to root out of the people's minds every desire to return to the worship of idols and to the comforts of an easier life. Anyone can see that these characteristics represent values common to all who claim Abraham as their father. Jews and Christians will admit this readily, while at the same time pointing out certain essential differences. The Qur'anic narrative does not mention the tenth plague nor the Passover which is derived from it as the decisive event in Jewish history and the primary liturgical institution of Judaism. Neither does it record the reciprocal requirements involved in the Covenant made at Sinai between God and the people chosen by Him. However, the substance of the Decalogue is found in the Qur'an.

3. Jesus[5]

Jesus (*'Isa*) is described in the Qur'an as having been placed beforehand under the "protection" of God against "Satan the outcast." This occurred when Mary, His mother, was born, since He was "her offspring" (Qur'an 3:36), declared by John to be "truly a Word emanating from God" (Qur'an 3:39). Jesus' birth was announced to Mary by the Spirit, who "assumed for her the likeness of a perfect man," and announced that her son would be "a revelation for mankind and a mercy from Us" (Qur'an 19:17–21). Mary is seen as "she who was chaste. . . . We breathed into her (something) of Our spirit and made her and her son a token for (all) peoples" (Qur'an 21:91). "Allah createth what He will" (Qur'an 3:47). To describe the mystery of Jesus' origin the Qur'an employs two narratives of the Annunciation and one of the Nativity (Qur'an 19:17–21; 3:42–47; 19:22–33). For Jesus God had formed the plan to "teach him the Scripture and wisdom, and the Torah and the Gospel" (Qur'an 3:48).

Thus Jesus came in the line of the prophets, "to follow in their footsteps, confirming that which was (revealed) before him, and We bestowed on him the Gospel wherein is guidance and a light" (Qur'an 5:46). He was sent as "a messenger unto the children of Israel" to bring them "a sign" from their Lord (Qur'an 3:49). He made "lawful some of that which was forbidden" to them (Qur'an 3:50). The "clear proofs" (Qur'an 43:63) and miraculous signs of His mission were numberless. Even at His birth He spoke to His mother "from below her" and to all those around Him when he was still "in the cradle" (Qur'an 19:24–29). He molded birds of clay and gave them life, healed the blind and the leper, raised the dead, etc. (Qur'an 3:49; 5:110). Then in answer to His prayer, God sent down from heaven for His disciples "a table spread with food from heaven," that it might serve as a feast "for the first" as well as "for the last" of them (Qur'an 5:112–115). His message was very simple, for He exhorted His people to worship God who is "my Lord and your Lord," because "that is a straight path," so "keep your duty to Allah and obey me" (Qur'an 3:50–51). "I have come to you with wisdom, and to make plain some of that concerning which you differ" (Qur'an 43:63).

Things came to a dramatic end when Jesus, becoming "conscious of their disbelief," and realizing that His disciples were "helpers in the cause of Allah" (Qur'an 3:52,53), cursed the Jews (Qur'an 5:78) and committed Himself to God, "the best of schemers" (Qur'an 3:54). In fact, according to the Qur'anic text, Jesus escaped defeat and death, for, "Allah said: O Jesus! Lo! I am gathering thee and causing thee to ascend unto Me, and am cleansing thee of those who disbelieve" (Qur'an 3:55). The Jews had said, "We slew the Messiah son of Mary, Allah's messenger—They slew him not nor crucified, but it appeared so unto them. . . . They slew him not for certain. But Allah took him up unto Himself" (Qur'an 4:157). All Muslims, then, affirm that Jesus is still living, and many believe that He is the key to "knowledge of the Hour" (Qur'an 43:61) of final judgment, that He will return as a Muslim to "witness against" the People of Scripture on the Day of Resurrection (Qur'an 4:159), after having experienced death like other mortals, thus fulfilling the verse: "Peace on me the day

I was born and the day I die, and the day I shall be raised alive!" (Qur'an 19:33).

Such is the extraordinary description of the person of Jesus in the Qur'an. He is "Messiah Jesus, son of Mary" (Qur'an 4:157), both prophet and messenger, a "faultless" "slave of Allah" (Qur'an 19:19,30), who could say that God "hath made me blessed . . . and (hath made me) dutiful toward her who bore me, and hath not made me arrogant, unblest" (Qur'an 19:31,32). He received generously from the divine "bounty" (Qur'an 4:173). He was, like Adam, created directly by God, and His coming was announced by John the forerunner (Qur'an 3:39). As a "word from Allah," "conveyed unto Mary" (Qur'an 4:171), Jesus' birth resulted from an action of the "Spirit" which God sent to her (Qur'an 19:17), and His life was sustained by that same "holy Spirit" (Qur'an 2:87). "The Messiah, Jesus, son of Mary, was only a messenger of Allah, and His word, which He conveyed unto Mary, and a spirit from Him" (Qur'an 4:171).

The Qur'an also points out that God "hath taken neither wife nor son" (Qur'an 72:3), for "He begetteth not nor was begotten" (Qur'an 112:3). It is also said that those who say, "Allah is the Messiah, son of Mary," are unbelievers (Qur'an 5:17), even as are those who say, "Allah is the third of three" (Qur'an 5:73). "O People of the Scripture . . . say not 'Three'—Cease!" (Qur'an 4:171). Then another verse seems to place Mary with God and Jesus to constitute a strange trinity: "And when Allah saith: O Jesus, son of Mary! Didst thou say unto mankind: Take me and my mother for two gods beside Allah? he saith: Be glorified! It was not mine to utter that to which I had no right. If I used to say it, then Thou knewest it. Thou knowest what is in my mind, and I know not what is in Thy mind" (Qur'an 5:116).

Christians can only rejoice over the fact that the Qur'an presents Jesus and his virgin mother as "portent . . . for (all) peoples" (Qur'an 21:91 and 23:50). Some Muslims have even gone so far as to consider Jesus as the "seal of holiness." Nevertheless, Christian belief regarding the person and mission of Jesus, based on the experience of the Apostles with him, transmitted and put into practice by the Church, is quite different from the Muslim belief. While recognizing with joy the position of greatness and of privilege granted to Jesus by the Qur'an, Christians are also aware of the fundamental differences which separate Muslim belief from the Christian belief in Jesus as Son of God and God Himself. In the Qur'an there is neither baptism nor Easter, divine epiphany nor victory over death, but simply a prophetic ministry described with particular emphasis on material found in the non-canonical Gospels. These differences notwithstanding, Christians should consider positively the degree to which the figure of Jesus in the Qur'an provides a striking analogy with the affirmations of their Scriptures, and they should welcome the great interest which Muslims show, even at the present time, in the person of the Messiah, the holiness of his life and the sublimity of his message.

Finally, it should be pointed out how much the Qur'anic picture of Mary, the mother of Jesus, encourages a feeling of respect by Muslims for her person and mission. The Qur'an speaks of her "nativity," her "withdrawal to the Temple," the "annunciation," the "nativity of Jesus," the "calumny" endured by the Virgin Mary, and the "ultimate meaning" of her life. Mary, as well as her "offspring," was placed under divine "protection" (Qur'an 3:36). Some hadith even affirm that Jesus and his mother alone were wholly without sin. The angels said to her, "O Mary! Lo! Allah hath chosen thee and made thee pure, and hath preferred thee above (all) the women of creation" (Qur'an 3:42). She is, then, a believing, pious virgin. With her son, she is "a token for (all) peoples" (Qur'an 21:91), for "We breathed therein something of Our Spirit. And she put faith in the words of her Lord and His Scriptures, and was of the obedient" (Qur'an 66:12). Thus it is fitting for believers of every generation to exalt Mary, the perfect woman, the one in whom God accomplished great things, because she was willing to be the "handmaid of the Lord" (Luke 1:38).

4. Muhammad[6]

The last of the prophetic models presented in the Qur'an is as well the most perfect one, the most definitive one, to Muslims, for he is the "seal of the prophets" (*khatam al-anbiya'*). The confession of this truth constitutes part of the Islamic creed: "I witness that Muhammad is the Messenger of God." In a way, the mission of Muhammad sums up those of previous prophets and presents itself as their fulfillment. Of course, "Muhammad is but a messenger, messengers (the like of whom) have passed away before him" (Qur'an 3:144), and God enjoins him to say to his people, "I am only a mortal like you. It is inspired in me that your God is One God, therefore take the straight path unto Him and seek forgiveness of Him" (Qur'an 41:6). Repeatedly it is said to him, "O Prophet! Lo! We have sent thee as a witness and a bringer of good tidings and a warner, and as a summoner unto Allah by His permission, and as a lamp that giveth light. And announce unto the believers the good tidings that they will have great bounty from Allah" (Qur'an 33:45–47). Frequently the Qur'an recalls the blessings that Muhammad has enjoyed from God. "Thy Lord hath not forsaken thee nor doth He hate thee. . . . Did He not find thee an orphan and protect (thee)? Did He not find thee wandering and direct (thee)? Did He not find thee destitute and enrich (thee)? . . . Therefore of the bounty of thy Lord be thy discourse" (Qur'an 93:3–11). "Have we not eased thee of the burden which weighed down thy back; and exalted thy fame?" (Qur'an 94:2–4).

The Qur'an often reminds this final messenger of the nature of his mission. "Make known that which hath been revealed unto thee from thy Lord" (Qur'an 5:67), for the Qur'an "is a revelation of the Lord of the Worlds, which the True Spirit hath brought down upon thy heart, that thou mayest be (one) of the warners, in plain Arabic speech" (Qur'an 26:192–195). "Say: My Lord inspireth in me that your God is only One God. And whoever hopeth for the meeting with his Lord, let him do righteous work, and make none sharer of the worship due unto his Lord" (Qur'an 18:110). In order to carry out that mission worthily Muhammad was endowed with extraordinary privileges and was given particular prescriptions for his people, regarding worship, law, family status and personal behavior. Perhaps the most eminent favor that was granted to him was what is called the "Night Journey" and the "Ascension," of which the Qur'an says, "Glorified be He Who carried His servant by night from the Inviolable Place of Worship to the Far Distant Place of Worship the neighborhood whereof We have blessed, that We might show him of Our tokens" (Qur'an 17:1). It is no doubt by virtue of such privilege that all authority has been given him, as the Qur'an says, "Obey Allah and obey the messenger, and beware" (Qur'an 5:92)! God "hath sent His messenger with the guidance and the religion of Truth, that He may cause it to prevail over all religion" (Qur'an 48:28).

The role of Muhammad proves, then, to be decisive for Muslims, since they consider it to be the final stage of revelation. Since he was "of a tremendous nature" (Qur'an 68:4), and since Muslims agree that "in the messenger of Allah ye have a good example" (Qur'an 33:21), it was natural that his Companions and the ones who followed them (the Followers) should have taken great care to collect and to transmit his acts, his words and his silences, all of which together became the "prophetic sayings" (hadith), which constituted thereafter the Tradition (*Sunna*). As the years passed the number of sayings grew until such time, in the ninth century, when a first great effort of criticism took place and the mass of material was stabilized in a definitive corpus. In their way the hadith witness to the growing importance of the prophetic model in the eyes of Muslims. By means of the multiple chains of transmitters and the different versions of each saying, the community sought, and seeks today, to clarify the behavior and the teaching of Muhammad as the supreme model of the Islamic ideal.

This elevation of the prophetic model, emphasized by Qur'anic exhortations, explains why popular devotion and mystical meditation have led Muslims, in a spirit of full admiration and veneration, to give indefectible loyalty to Muhammad. Sometimes they even call upon him for intercession. Some have elaborated a long litany of two hundred Beautiful Names of Muhammad to express their piety. Many celebrate the annual festival which commemorates "the birth of the Prophet" (*Al-Mawlid al-Nabawi*), the twelfth of the month of Rabi' al-awwal. Among the religious brotherhoods there is an emphasis upon the mediation of the Prophet in order to justify the holiness of their founders. Certain mystics have gone so far as to uplift the "Muhammadan light" and its role as archetype in the beginnings of history. Likewise the ceremonies of pilgrimage to Mecca have been amplified to include a pious visit to the tomb of the Prophet in Medina.

Christians should have all of the foregoing in mind when they have occasion to speak of Muhammad. Without always having to distinguish between the "Muhammad of history" and the "Muhammad of faith," they should fully respect the deep affection which Muslims feel and manifest toward their Prophet. It should be pointed out that Muslims are often saddened to see that their Christian friends do not grant him the status of prophet, whereas, for their part, they recognize that quality in Jesus. As Christians become aware of this difficulty in the minds of Muslims they will wish to go further into it on the basis of differing understandings of what is meant by prophecy in the fullest sense. Christians should try to appreciate the authentic value of the life and work of the Prophet of Islam, taking into consideration the time and the environment in which he lived. They must renounce firmly "all the occasions where lack of respect has been shown, where incorrect statements in speech or in writing have been made, where unhelpful, even insulting, suggestions have been offered with reference to Muhammad, the venerated Prophet of Islam."[7] Instead of these negative judgments which came out of former concern for polemics and apologetics, Christians should assess in an objective way, and in consonance with their faith, exactly what was the inspiration, the sincerity and the faithfulness of the Prophet Muhammad, making their judgment within the framework, first, of his personal response to the commands of God, and then, on a wider scale, that of the working of providence in world history.

Respecting the requirements of dialogue, both parties need to take into consideration their differing definitions of prophethood in the fullest sense. So, Christians will not require that Muslims recognize in Jesus all of the qualities which Christianity has conferred upon him (Word and Son of God, redeemer and savior, "first-born of all creation"). And, in like manner, a Muslim should not require that a Christian recognize in Muhammad all of the qualities that Islam has attributed to him (Seal of the prophets, infallibility and sinlessness). Christians are inclined to perceive that Muhammad was a great literary, political and religious genius, and that he possessed particular qualities which enabled him to lead multitudes to the worship of the true God. But, at the same time, they find in him evidence of certain mistakes and important misapprehensions. They also discern in him marks of prophethood. "His faith in the One God is a constant of his message and of his life . . . his call for justice and for human dignity is a cry that cannot be silenced."[8] In expressing this perception they can use the appropriate words which the Patriarch Timothy of Baghdad uttered long ago in an exchange with the Caliph of his time: "Muhammad followed the way of the prophets,"[9] for he surely conformed to their example, without, however, corresponding fully to the One whom they foretold.

IV
THE SOLIDARITY OF A COMMUNITY
OF BELIEVERS

Since Muslims are conscious of belonging to "the best community that hath been raised up for mankind" (Qur'an 3:110), they feel the vital necessity of remaining united in faith and action. "Hold fast, all of you together, to the cable of Allah, and do not separate. And remember Allah's favour unto you" (Qur'an 3:103). And, in fact, one of the primary expressions of divine favor is that "maternal community" (*Umma*) which forms them, nourishes them, permeates, surrounds, supports and exalts them. It is the "house of Islam" (*Dar al-Islam*) which is also the "house of justice and of peace" (*Dar al-'adl wa-l-salam*), a unified society in which all members feel very close to each other, regardless of their differences in race, language or civilization. Many hadith underscore the value and grandeur of this "community conscience." It is constantly affirmed that "the believers are naught else than brothers" (Qur'an 49:10), and at the same time it is insisted in the hadith that "no one is a true believer who does not desire for his brother that which he desires for himself." This means that all Muslims are brothers and sisters. They do not oppress one another, abandon one another, lie to one another or despise one another. Everything pertaining to a Muslim is sacred to another Muslim: blood, possessions and honor.

Thus it is by being members of the Community of the Prophet (*Ummat al-Nabi*) that all Muslims understand themselves to be believers (*mu'minun*) and submitted to God (*muslimun*). Islam being both a blueprint for civilization and a religious experience, the community takes on a very human visage for believers, with historical dimensions through which they can project the full development of an Islam in which "religion and state" (*din wa-dawla*) are joined in perfect harmony. The great historical civilizations of Islam are considered to have been successful attempts to organize society according to the Islamic pattern, giving full opportunity for the flourishing of arts and letters, science, culture, philosophy and theology. This success is acknowledged to have been dependent, however, upon the incorporation of foreign elements from Greece, India, the Byzantine Empire, China and Europe. Those great civilizations of the past deeply mark the "community memory" of Islam today, and give impetus to the desire of the eight hundred million Muslims in this fifteenth century of the hijra to live together in unity. Theirs is not a paralyzing nostalgia, but a utopian vision ever renewed, reminding all that there is an Islamic way for organizing society, of developing economic life, of permitting a humanism of believers to flourish, with a variety of schools of thought, tendencies and even sects, since "divergence is also a mercy," as a hadith says.

This community is all the more longed for by Muslims by virtue of the comforting support which it gives them when they meet each Friday noon at the mosque for congregational prayer, and especially when they assemble annually at Mecca, nearly two million pilgrims from the whole world, gathered there to reflect upon what Islam means to them. The community guarantees to the believers security and even infallibility. A hadith affirms that "my community will never agree upon an error." This is why most theologians and jurists have considered that the unanimous consensus (*ijma'*) of the community constitutes the third source of Islamic thought, after the Qur'an and the Hadith. It is also why the Sunnis like to call themselves *Ahl al-Jama'a* (The People of the Community). Besides being a safeguard of orthodox faith, the community also provides fraternal support for action by the practice of "commanding the right" (*al-amr bi-l-ma'ruf*), even as the Qur'an recommends: "And let there be from you a nation who invite to goodness, and enjoin right conduct and forbid indecency" (Qur'an 3:104).

V
TESTIMONY TO THE TRANSCENDENCE OF GOD[10]

The clear affirmation of the transcendence of God is the hallmark of Islam, making each believer a witness (*shahid*) of the universal lordship of God, and possibly, if the necessity arises, making a martyr (*shahid*) of the witness. Thus Muslims follow the example of the prophets who, throughout history, insisted that "He is Allah, the One! . . . And there is none comparable unto Him" (Qur'an 112:1–4).

With the conviction of the absolute transcendence of their Lord, Muslims receive from Him the revelation of His oneness (*tawhid*), and they make it the model of their lives, becoming both its defenders and its servants. They know that God is at the same time both completely other than they and very close to them, since, on the one hand, "with Him are the keys of the invisible. None but He knoweth them" (Qur'an 6:59), and, on the other hand, He is nearer to them than their jugular vein (see Qur'an 50:16). Islamic thought has developed what might be called a negative theology in which the divine mystery remains forever inaccessible to human understanding. Al-Ghazali, the eleventh-century theologian, questions the believer: "What is the utmost limit to which the initiated can arrive in their knowledge of God? It is precisely their inability to understand Him. Their true knowledge is to perceive that they do not know Him and that they cannot, in any way, know Him, since to know God truly is impossible for anyone other than God Himself!"[11]

Fortunately for Muslim believers, God has spoken of Himself in the Qur'an, and it is by reading it carefully that they are able to draw out of it the "Ninety-nine Beautiful Names" of God, which are like a partial shining forth of the mystery of the One God. "Allah's are the fairest names. Invoke Him by them" (Qur'an 7:180). "He is Allah. . . . He is the Beneficent, the Merciful. . . . He is the Sovereign Lord, the Holy One, Peace, the Keeper of Faith, the Guardian, the Majestic, the Compeller, the Superb . . . the Creator, the Shaper out of naught, the Fashioner . . . the Mighty, the Wise" (Qur'an 59:22–24). By repeatedly saying the thirty-three beads of their chaplet (*subha*) three times, Muslims learn its litany by heart. Sometimes they group all of the Beautiful Names around the essential attributes of the Lord: creation and greatness, providence and mercy, justice and retribution, and by such an exercise they feel closer to the greatest of the Names, Allah (God Himself). They perceive that "Allah is the Light of the heavens and the earth. . . . Light upon light, Allah guideth unto His light whom He will" (Qur'an 24:35).

Thanks to this illumination, the Muslim's expression of faith develops at all levels: the witness of the heart to a deep commitment, the witness of the tongue in confessing the faith, and the witness of the whole person by carrying out the deeds prescribed by the faith. The different theological schools of thought are not agreed as to whether faith alone can save, without works, but it is certainly accepted everywhere that by pronouncing the *shahada* (confession of faith), a person is received into the community and gains access to the mercy of God.

It is natural that both Christians and Muslims should think that they have much to say to one another about the divine mystery, since the Bible of the Christians is full of wonderful Names for God, of evocative parables and meaningful revelations. Both groups consider themselves as servants of the transcendent deity and witnesses of the Eternal in a world where idol worship is forever reappearing and where the greatness of humankind is sometimes made to rest on the declaration of the "death of God." For their part, Christians consider Muslims "with esteem. They adore one God, living and enduring, merciful and all-powerful, Maker of heaven and earth and Speaker to men . . . [and] await the day of judgment when God will give each man his due after raising him up" (*Nostra Aetate,* No. 3).

VI
SOBER RITES OF WORSHIP[12]

Muslims intend to demonstrate by their worship (*'ibada*) that they are servants of God (*'ibad* [sing. *'abd*] *Allah*), and that they are responding to the primordial design of the Creator, who said, "I created the jinn and humankind only that they might worship Me" (Qur'an 51:56). In the hadith it is pointed out that "Islam has been erected on five pillars: witness that there is no god but God and that Muhammad is the Messenger of God; doing prayer; contributing to charity; observing the fast of the month of Ramadan; carrying out the pilgrimage to the holy House, when it is possible to do so." All of these rites have as their first and last purpose the glory and praise of the One God, for they constitute the "best forms of worship" and the "best form of service" to the One who alone is worthy of being the "First Served." Everywhere it is known that the Muslim community is made up of men and women who alike confess the faith, pray, fast, give to charity and do the pilgrimage (these are the five "pillars" of Islam).

Ritual prayer (*salat*) must be performed five times each day, corresponding to the important turns of the day (dawn, noon, afternoon, sunset and evening). It is preceded by either partial or complete ablutions, depending upon whether the worshiper is in a state of minor or major impurity. The prayer is composed of bodily movements and simple words which express the complete submission of the Muslim to God. The daily fast (*siyam*) of the month of Ramadan gives the worshiper an opportunity to experience hunger, thirst and abstinence as an offering given to God. Ramadan is a collective retreat of the Muslim community, during which multiplied prayers and nocturnal meditations are offered to Him who is Divine Providence. The compulsory contribution to charity (*zakat*), or the optional one (*sadaqa*), permits the believers to share with the poor and needy the material goods which they have acquired and to purify by that means their use of that which remains. The pilgrimage (*hajj*) to Mecca takes them back to the sources of their faith and history, gives supranational dimensions to their religious experience, and, especially, prepares them for and leads them to the grace of contrition and forgiveness, through the various stages of a true conversion to God.

Everyone knows that this worship must be sincere and carried out in a spirit of ihsan, "which means to serve God as though you see Him, because, even if you do not see Him, He sees you" (hadith). "The value of works lies only in the intention (*niyya*)" (hadith). So, those who would worship and give thanks can only do so with pure heart and converted mind. In fact the Qur'an repeatedly condemns those who try to "negotiate" with God hypocritically (munafiqun) or ostentatiously (*mura'un*). For this reason Muslims seek to emphasize the inner dimensions of their worship in order to discover the hidden purposes of God.

At this juncture Christians are encouraged by the Second Vatican Council to respect the sincere worship of the living God by Muslims. Even though the forms and ceremonies of their prayer, fasting, almsgiving and pilgrimage differ in various ways, Muslims and Christians are conscious that they possess in common certain ancient practices of invocation, litany, intercession, meditation and retreat, and that by means of these they renew continually their spiritual energy and moral strength. Sometimes the shared desire to call upon God together even leads them, by common accord, to draw words and gestures from their respective traditions to express their immediate joint feeling before God; and they do this without minimizing the long-established formal rites of their particular ways of worship.

VII
OBEDIENCE AND FAITHFULNESS
TO THE PRESCRIPTIONS OF THE LAW[13]

True Muslims know that faith without works would be neither authentic nor acceptable to God. A famous verse reminds them that "it is not righteousness that ye turn your faces to the East and the West; but righteous is he who believeth in Allah and the Last Day and the angels and the Scripture and the Prophets; and giveth his wealth, for love of Him, to kinsfolk and to orphans and the needy and the wayfarer and to those who ask, and to set slaves free; and observeth proper worship and payeth the poor-due. And those who keep their treaty when they make one, and the patient in tribulation and adversity and time of stress. Such are they who are sincere. Such are the Godfearing" (Qur'an 2:177). So it is by doing all that is possible to be righteous and by strictly obeying the commands of God that Muslims find their equilibrium as human beings and their spiritual satisfaction. They realize that although "Allah sendeth whom He will astray, and guideth whom He will" (Qur'an 14:4), it is also true that humans must freely choose their destiny, for God has said, "Then whosoever will, let him believe, and whosoever will, let him disbelieve" (Qur'an 18:29). Conscious of these two parallel truths Muslims are able to situate their responsibility within the mysterious interplay between divine predestination and human freedom. And since their holy book points out in certain areas what is the specific will of God regarding human behavior, they have only to deduce from the book the fundamental principles and the particular applications of divine law (*shari'a*), and turn to jurisprudence (*fiqh*) for its authoritative interpretation.

Thus obedience to the commands of God and love for His law lead Muslims to find in the Qur'an, especially in its many legal verses, the essential features of all codes, whether domestic, economic, political, contractual or penal. To them it is an act of worship in praise of God's will to study His law constantly and to put its prescriptions into practice scrupulously. The zeal that many Muslims show for the divine law and the satisfaction that they find in it remind us of the attitudes expressed in Psalm 119 of the Bible. Finally it will be in terms of this same obedience that God, who is "swift at reckoning" (Qur'an 2:202), will reward everyone at the Day of Judgment, when "whoso doth good an atom's weight will see it then, and whoso doth ill an atom's weight will see it then" (Qur'an 99:7,8).

Muslims know also that their "mission" (*amana*) which the heavens and the earth "shrank from bearing" (Qur'an 33:72) is not always easy, nor is it ever finally accomplished. "Lo! man was created anxious" (Qur'an 33:72), "a wrong-doer, an ingrate" (Qur'an 14:34) and even "a tyrant and a fool" (Qur'an 33:72). This is why human beings sense a dramatic conflict in their personal lives between good and evil, a tension in which, ever since the sin of Adam, Satanic powers have been involved with human disobedience. Men and women find within themselves a soul that "enjoineth unto evil" (Qur'an 12:53) and, again, an "accusing soul" (Qur'an 75:2). Like many people, Muslims experience the bitterness of sin, and their theology has had to determine what is the position in the community of a "sinning believer." However, their hope is based on the immense goodness of God, since "He hath prescribed for Himself mercy" (Qur'an 6:12), and, according to a hadith, He has said, "My mercy prevails over My wrath." This is why the Qur'an often repeats to the believers, "Ask pardon of your Lord and then turn unto Him (repentant).

Lo! my Lord is Merciful, loving" (Qur'an 11:90). When finally the conflict between acceptance and refusal is over, and when the certainty of forgiveness is felt, Muslims hope to hear these words, "Ah! thou soul at peace! Return unto thy Lord, content in His good pleasure! Enter thou among My bondmen! Enter thou My Garden!" (Qur'an 89:27–30).

For the Christians' part, they endeavor so to live that "the will of the Father" might be done "on earth as it is in heaven" (Matthew 6:10). Thus they are able to understand the determined effort of their Muslim friends, who "strive to submit wholeheartedly even to His inscrutable decrees" (*Nostra Aetate,* No. 3), to appreciate their concern not only to know those decrees, but to understand them and to put them into practice, even though they as Christians believe that this can be accomplished within the framework of a universal law valid always and everywhere.

VIII
ASCETICAL AND MYSTICAL ACHIEVEMENTS[14]

It has been seen how the Muslim religious experience involves the confession of faith, the observance of worship and obedience to the law. Sometimes it happens that believers in their intense devotion desire to give more in response to God and to go a little further in their grasp of the faith. This can lead to a deep inner perception of worship and obedience that unfolds some of their ultimate meanings, as the believers seek humbly to imitate the attributes of their Lord. Accordingly their spiritual masters, such as Al-Ghazali, following the counsel of a hadith, call upon them to "put on the virtues of God (*al-takhalluq bi-akhlaq Allah*) because the perfection of believers is found in drawing near to their Lord in order to take on some of His praise-worthy attributes: knowledge, righteousness, goodness, kindness, beneficence, mercy, good counsel, exhortation to do good and warning against doing evil."[15] This undertaking is made possible by a mysterious likeness which is affirmed by the hadith: "God created Adam in His image."

It is evident that many have tried, by going methodically through stages of renunciation and self-denial, of imitation and compliance, to achieve a certain intimacy with their Lord. The history of Islam witnesses to the fact that among Muslims there has been no lack of those who, through the centuries, have practiced a sober asceticism and a quest for mystical experience.[16]

Muslim mysticism (*tasawwuf*) has not always been accepted as orthodox by the Islamic community as a whole, but it has nevertheless provided many believers with methods, processes and models whereby they can hope to participate, either intimately or as observers, in what is called "the unity of witness," or "the unity of existence." Achievements in the mystical field have been abundantly attested, and religious orders were formed to make them accessible even to the masses of ordinary believers. It is perhaps at this high level of approach to the divine mystery that there ought to be more exchanges between certain individuals. After all, twenty centuries of Christian life and fourteen centuries of Muslim life represent a unique capital of religious experience and mystical quest, wherein human holiness is considered to be the choicest gift that God has given to humanity.

The Islamic values of faith and worship that have been described in this chapter will certainly call forth respect, understanding and sympathy on the part of Christians when they see them embodied in the lives of Muslims. The declaration *Nostra Aetate* of the Second Vatican Council, concerning the relations of the Church with non-Christian religions, states, "Upon the Muslims, too, the Church looks with esteem. They adore one God, living and enduring, merciful and all-powerful, Maker of heaven and earth and Speaker to men. They strive to submit wholeheartedly even to His inscrutable decrees, just as did Abraham, with whom the Islamic faith is pleased to associate itself. Though they do not acknowledge Jesus as God, they revere Him as a prophet. They also honor Mary, His virgin mother; at times they call on her, too, with devotion. In addition they await the day of judgment when God will give each man his due after raising him up. Consequently, they prize the moral life, and give worship to God especially through prayer, almsgiving, and fasting" (No. 3). Because of this respect the same Second Vatican Council was able to declare that "the plan of salvation also includes those who acknowledge the Creator. In the first place among these there are the Muslims, who, professing to hold the faith of Abraham, along with us adore the one and merciful God, who on the last day will judge mankind" (*Lumen Gentium,* Ch. II, No. 16).

Thus Christian thought is invited to give Islam a special place as a monotheistic, prophetic religion which is linked with the Judeo-Christian tradition. It can be understood in the following ways: (1) as one of the many great human expressions of the search for God through complete submission (*islam*) and a disciplined life of worship; (2) as a particular preparation for meeting the God of Abraham, Moses and Jesus; (3) as a place of privilege where access is gained to divine mercy and, thence, to salvation; (4) as a providentially provided historical intermediary whose adherents, by the example of their righteous lives, point the way to the blessings of divine grace.

It is not necessary to go further into the details of various Christian theological evaluations of Islam, its Book and its Prophet. It is enough to respect the diversity of such interpretations, that is, as long as they are founded on scientific conclusions and theologically coherent principles. Whatever theological explanation is given, Christians can and should consider their Muslim friends as true witnesses of the living God, and their religion as a fervent appropriation of the message originally given to Abraham. Muslims take him as the model of faith and submission for all of humankind. His message and example provide a potential meeting place for all believers in the One God where they might be fully reconciled to each other. It would seem that today Jews, Muslims and Christians are called upon to "bless themselves by him" together and to help each other become in the future true "children of Abraham," and "do what Abraham did." This is no doubt the sense of the following statement by the Second Vatican Council: "Although in the course of the centuries many quarrels and hostilities have arisen between Christians and Muslims, this most sacred Synod urges all to forget the past and to strive sincerely for mutual understanding. On behalf of all mankind, let them make common cause of safeguarding and fostering social justice, moral values, peace, and freedom" (*Nostra Aetate,* No. 3).

Notes

1. See Bibliography; further, M. Talbi, "Foi d'Abraham et foi islamique," *Islamochristiana* 5 (1979), 1–5; English translation in *Encounter* (Documents for Muslim-Christian Understanding), Rome, No. 92, Feb. 1983.
2. See M. Talbi, note 1, and Y. Moubarac, *Abraham dans le Coran,* Paris: Vrin, 1958.
3. See especially Youakim Moubarac, *op. cit.*
4. For nearly three centuries Islamic tradition hesitated between Isaac and Ishmael before finally deciding upon the latter. On this question see Jean Fontaine, "Ibn Khaldun, chercheur indépendant dans la question du Dhabih Allah," in IBLA (Tunis), No. 116, 4me trim., 1966, pp. 421–432; Michel Hayek, *Le mystère d'Ismaël,* Paris: Mame, 1964; and Rene Dagorn, *La geste d'Ismaël d'après l'onomastique et la tradition arabes,* Genève: Droz and Paris: Champion, 1981.
5. See in Bibliography, G. Parrinder; also J.M. Abd-el-Jalil, *Marie et l'Islam,* Paris: Beauchesne, 1950; M. Hayek, *Le Christ de l'Islam,* Paris: Seuil, 1959; M.L. Fitzgerald, "Jesus: a Sign for Christians and Muslims," *Encounter,* 72 (1981); J. McL. Ritchie, "Christianity in the Qur'an," *Encounter* 81 (1982); "Christ seen by contemporary Muslim writers" (English translation from *Se Comprendre*), *Encounter* 87 (1982).
6. See Section III of the Bibliography.
7. Jacques Lanfry. "What must we do to combat the prejudices and misunderstandings that separate us?" Document C of "Muslim-Christian Congress, Tripoli, 1–6 February, 1976," in *Current Documentations,* 5, April 1976 (published by the White Fathers' Documentation Office in Rome).
8. From the first part of the "Allocution inaugurale" by Cardinal Tarancon at the Second Christian-Muslim meeting at Cordoba (March 1977). The whole text is published in *Documentation Catholique* (Paris), No. 1720, May 15, 1977, pp. 480–483.
9. Cf. Robert Caspar, "Les versions arabes du Dialogue entre le Catholicos Timothée I et

le calife al-Mehdi (IIe/VIII/siecle): 'Muhammad a suivi la voie des prophètes' " (introduction, critical edition and translation), *Islamochristiana* 3 (1977), 107–175. H. Putman, *L'Eglise et l'Islam sous Timothée* (780–823), Beirut: Dar al Mashriq, 1975 (1977).
    10. See the article, "Allah," in *Encyclopaedia of Islam,* New Edition.
    11. Abu Hamid al-Ghazali, *Al-Maqsad al-asna fi sharh asma' Allah al-husna (Commentary on the Beautiful Names of God).* Cairo: Maktabat al-Kulliya al-Azhariya, n.d., p. 28.
    12. Besides the basic works mentioned in the Bibliography, see Maurice Borrmans, "Rites et culte en Islam," *Studia Missionalia,* Rome, Vol. 23, 1974, pp. 161–190; Mohammed Talbi, "A Muslim Experience of Prayer," *Encounter,* 34 (1977).
    13. On Muslim law see J. Schacht, *An Introduction to Islamic Law,* Oxford, Clarendon Press, 2nd ed., 1967; N.J. Coulson, *A History of Islamic Law,* Islamic Surveys 2, Edinburgh University Press, 1964; J.N.D. Anderson, *Islamic Law in the Modern World,* London, 1959; idem, *Law Reform in the Muslim World,* London, 1976.
    14. See Bibliography, especially Arberry, *Sufism,* and Nicholson.
    15. Abu Hamid al-Ghazali, *Ihya' 'ulum al-din* (Revival of Religious Sciences), Cairo: Al-Babi al-Halabi, 1358/1939, vol. 4, p. 298.
    16. Examples are Hasan al-Basri (642–728), the "mystic of the city"; Rabi'a al-'Adawiyya (713–801), "poetess of pure love"; Al-Muhasibi (781–857), the "master of self-examination"; Al-Junayd (d. 910), the "wise spiritual counselor"; Al-Bistami (d. 874), "witness of absolute unity"; Al-Hallaj (858–922), the witness of "the union of love through great suffering"; and many others who lived later, whether in Spain, such as Ibn 'Arabi (1165–1240), or in Egypt, such as Ibn al-Farid (1181–1235), or, especially in Persia, such as Suhrawardi (1151–1191), bearer of "enlightening wisdom," and Jalal al-Din al-Rumi (1207–1273), singer of "mystical poetry."

Chapter Four
Dealing with Present Obstacles

Believers cannot be content simply to investigate by faith the various possibilities for dialogue that exist and to recognize freely the religious values which make up the life and witness of each group. They realize that their dialogue takes place in a history whose past eludes them, but which at the same time envelops and conditions them. They are marked by their particular national culture before they have a chance to make any contribution to it themselves. A part of this cultural heritage is the way that each religion has regarded the other. No one can escape the influence of this historical image of the other religion. So believers must struggle constantly against the pressure of their own background in order to distinguish those obstacles, both subjective and objective, which today reduce the chances for a true dialogue or which even risk blocking all efforts to come together in understanding.

I
RECOGNIZING AND THEN FORGETTING WRONGS OF THE PAST[1]

If Christians and Muslims should draw up a list of misunderstandings, hostilities and injustices that have accumulated through the fourteen centuries of their more or less common history, they would certainly lose heart, for the long list would contain legitimate accusations and justified grievances put forward in perfectly good faith by both sides.

There would be first of all the long series of political and cultural confrontations with the Byzantines and later the Europeans, struggles that coincided with the beginnings of Islamic civilization, its time of highest development, its long decline and then its present revival. Christians should realize that in general Muslims believe themselves to have been unjustly humiliated in both the political and the cultural spheres during the past centuries. This feeling should be duly noted and a deliberate effort should be made to investigate its causes and manifestations.

Christians need to explain these enmities of the past, taking into account that economic, ideological and political factors were just as important in them, if not more important, than religious factors. They should encourage their Muslim partners to seek, through self-criticism, a more equitable assessment of relative responsibility on the part of each of the two religions for the tragic events of their common history. Those events should be studied in an atmosphere of mutual consultation and sound historical criticism, so that, through a joint reinterpretation of them, any tendentious or even dishonest appeal to religious values might be avoided.

By dissociating Christian and Muslim religious values from the injustices of the past which believers have committed in their name, or which have been falsely attributed to them, it is possible to imagine a willingness on the part of both parties to overlook any remaining ill effects of those injustices. This process of discernment must continue, for both Christians and Muslims need to apply it to the historical events of the present in which they are active participants.

A similar effort should be undertaken in the more specifically cultural and religious areas. Centuries of polemics have shown that honest and open discussion degenerated quickly into bitter criticism and contests of apologetics, even into accusations of an offensive nature and ridicule. Christians and Muslims have suffered from having their essential values misunderstood and misrepresented. From the Christian side, how many slanderous statements and insulting writings have been produced against Muhammad, the Prophet of Islam? And, from the Muslim side, how many careless statements and hasty judgments have been made regarding the Christian mysteries of the Trinity, the Incarnation and Redemption? Here again a joint, impartial investigation of these outmoded polemics will help prevent their use today and encourage the avoidance of arguments and displays that would be disrespectful of both the divine honor and the faith of believers. All should examine themselves to see if they are completely without blame in this respect!

It may be noted here that Muslims often suspect the work of the Orientalists as giving an interpretation of Islam that shares the prejudices of Western science against the Arab world and Islamic civilization. It is especially important that in Muslim-Christian dialogue Islam not be identified exclusively with Arab civilization, for the latter includes the important contribution of Arab Christians as well as that of Muslims. Likewise the West should not be considered as entirely Christian, because Christianity was born in the Middle East, and can never belong exclusively to one civilization. Also the West has evolved into a secular and pluralistic society. In order to make better use of the knowledge and interpretations of the Orientalists and Western Islamicists, Christians should make clear their position regarding the Muslim criticisms of their work. Christians might also encourage Muslims to increase, from their side, the number of scholars of Christianity who, with an objective understanding of true Christianity, might interpret to their coreligionists the ways in which Christians live their faith and desire to see it developed.

Finally, Muslims and Christians are both accused by modern atheists and secular humanists of having used religion, in both the past and the present, for ends that go against the honor of God and the dignity of humankind. It is true that believers in the two religions have sometimes minimized the gravity of political and economic injustices by supporting the status quo and ignoring the suffering of the poor. Sometimes religious traditions have been used to humiliate scholars by denying them the right to legitimate ambition and to needed research. Through a failure to appreciate the requirements of freedom and the autonomy of secular authority, religious people have sometimes arrogated for themselves power that has nothing to do with faith or charity. It has also happened that Christians and Muslims have appropriated the values of life, justice, brotherhood and peace for their own community alone, relegating religious minorities to a ghetto status, or requiring them to subscribe to politico-religious allegiance. Finally, the institution of slavery existing in the recent past can only give Christians and Muslims a bad conscience in relation to the peoples of black Africa, even considering that slavery was abolished more than a century ago. So, Christian and Muslim civilizations are not innocent before the judgment seat of history. It is good for believers to try humbly, but without complex, to draw lessons from the past that can be of benefit in the future.

II
ELIMINATION OF PREJUDICE[2]

Believers realize that they do not approach others without preconceived notions. Unfortunately, they share a whole cluster of ready-made ideas and images, inherited from their forebears or received from their community. These include arbitrary judgments and persistent prejudices that need to be corrected if the meeting with others and cooperation with them are to take place according to truth and charity. This applies even to areas of life that might seem not to fall under the influence of faith, such as science, technology and politics.

1. Is Islam Fatalistic?

Muslims glory in their submission to God and in their obedience to his law. Their confession of faith contains as its last article belief in divine predestination of both good and evil. In order better to exalt the greatness, power and omnipresence of God, Muslims have developed to a high degree, especially in ascetical and mystical circles, the virtues of renunciation, surrender to and confidence in God. Among the masses religious orders have sometimes encouraged an attitude akin to resignation in which the believer risks abandoning personal responsibility and denying the possibility of free choice with respect to God and other people. Islam has been accused of being the religion of *maktub* (it is decreed) and of teaching its believers to say too easily, "If God wills" (*In sha 'Allah*), "According to God's will" (*'Ala murad Allah*), or "God alone prevails" (*La ghaliba ill-Allah*).

Even so, it is not right to make Islam responsible for attitudes of excessive resignation that could lead to fatalism. Along with the long-predominant theological school of Ash'arism which tended to make the human being a mere "place" for the divine action, there was also the Mu'tazilite school which affirmed that human beings "create their deeds." In addition many modern Muslim thinkers continually insist that human deeds issue from a free and responsible moral agency, since God commands that people should use their intelligence and freedom to the utmost by practicing daily an "effort of personal interpretation" (*ijtihad*) in all matters where God has not given an explicit textual directive. And even a conclusive text requires some interpretation. This is what constitutes the greatness and responsibility of humankind before God. Many Muslims consider Islam as a "commitment" (*iltizam*) and a "supreme effort" (*jihad akbar*) to fulfill the will of God by working toward the perfecting of his work begun in creation. Thus Muslims demonstrate that their religion does not suppress human personality and freedom, but rather enhances them.

2. Is Islam Legalistic?

All religions run the risk of falling into legalism, since their message includes a moral code which necessarily must be expressed pedagogically for the masses in the form of commandments, including precepts and prohibitions. Islam, with the primary place it gives to law within its system, and with the detailed way in which prescriptions are given, might be said to provide well for the inner need of the religious consciousness for security. On the other hand, the classification of human acts into the "obligatory" (*wajib*), the "recommended" (*mustahabb*), the "permitted" (*mubah*), the "reprehensible" (*makruh*) and the "forbidden" (*haram*) can give rise to a spirit of moralizing legalism, especially if the ruling power seeks to enforce a certain moral order. And, in addition, many Muslims depend upon the above moral classification without going to the trouble to reflect on the basic goodness or evil of the things they do.

Nevertheless Muslims are always required to determine their "intention" (*niyya*) in order to discern the nature of their deeds and to carry them out humbly, in submission to God. Islamic "piety" (*birr*), rightly understood, is intended to bring believers to that spirit, since "acts of obedience" (*ta'at*) are seen as the first requirements of worship. So it would be completely unjust to claim that Islam is fundamentally legalistic or that it teaches believers they will automatically receive salvation simply by obeying the law.

3. Is Islam Morally Lax?

Being taught that they belong to the "community of the middle way" (Qur'an 2:143), Muslims believe that it is legitimate to give full satisfaction to all needs of their human nature, following particular guidelines for such fulfillment. When Christians compare those guidelines to the demands of the Gospel they judge too quickly that Muslims are morally lax, especially when they observe Muslim conduct that does not measure up to the ethical requirements of the Qur'an. There are many prejudices in this regard. Words like "harem" and "Muhammad's paradise" refer to pejorative judgments based on false interpretations of the facts and a lack of understanding.

There is a strict system of ethics (*akhlaq*) in Islam which is closely related to law in order that it might be more effectively observed. In its broad features, Islamic ethics is quite similar to the Ten Commandments given to Moses. So it would be wrong to say that there is no social morality for the Muslim family. Moral standards certainly exist, but they are different from those of the ideal Christian family. For example the Qur'an, tradition and most modern codes of law permit the Muslim husband to have two, three or four wives simultaneously, provided that he is equally just toward all of them (Qur'an 4:3). This requirement of equal justice has led several reformers, such as Muhammad 'Abduh and 'Allal al-Fasi, as well as certain nations, such as Turkey and Tunisia, to opt for and even legislate for the abolition of polygamy. Others have instituted strict limitations to the legal practice of having more than one wife. Then, with regard to divorce, this procedure is permitted by the Qur'an and so is recognized as the strict right of every Muslim husband. However, an often quoted hadith affirms that divorce is "of all permitted acts the most detestable to God." Many modern codes of family law restrict the practice of divorce and require careful judicial oversight of its procedures.

It should be recognized, then, that family life and conjugal morality are covered by regulations, and that these have evolved in recent years to grant more rights to women and children.[3] In another aspect of family life Islam has taken a very liberal course by permitting all methods of birth control. But it agrees with Christian morality in forbidding sterilization, refusing to accept abortion in most cases and condemning all forms of adultery, fornication and homosexuality. Conjugal faithfulness, love for children and respect for parents are values that Muslims recognize, practice, uplift and honor in appropriate ways.

As regards the Quranic descriptions of the joys of paradise, everything depends on the interpretation given to them. Many Muslims of the past and present, theologians, philosophers or mystics, regard those descriptions as only metaphorical, not to be taken literally. Of course Muslims believe that the future life will be quite similar to the present life, in that it will include all types of pleasures and joys to which soul and body are susceptible. But all realize that the chief joy of paradise will be: "That day will faces be resplendent, looking toward their Lord" (Qur'an 75:22, 23). Also a "divine" hadith affirms that "no one knows what God has prepared for His chosen ones, things unseen by any eye, unheard by any ear and unimagined by the human mind." And, just because the mercy of God is infinite and only the sin of unbelief or *kufr* (associating others with God) leads to eternal punishment, one should not conclude that the religion of Islam is easy, that Muslims' sins do not weigh heavily upon them. All that has just been said only confirms what was written previously about the full responsibility of believers before their Lord.

4. Is Islam Fanatical?

Muslims are often annoyed when they hear themselves accused of fanaticism and of having used force to make converts to their religion. They are quick to point out that Islam practices tolerance (*samaha*) and affirms that "there is no compulsion in religion" (Qur'an 2:256). When appropriate they quote verses from the Qur'an that show a favorable attitude toward Christians, and they recall the distinct benefits granted to the

People of Scripture by their "protected status" (*dhimmis*) in Islamic society of the classical period and in the Ottoman Empire. They do not have to look far in history to find excesses of Christian fanaticism, which make the occasions of Muslim fanaticism seem less blameworthy. If the stereotype of Muslim fanaticism remains very strong among Christians, however, it may be because there are in certain parts of the Islamic world examples of social pressure and communal solidarity that non-Muslims interpret as forms of latent intolerance. However, it should be remembered that in every mixed society the relationship of majority to minority is subject to sociological dynamics that do not necessarily involve the faith of the various peoples.

Here again Christians need to learn precisely what is the Islamic point of view regarding the world and faith. Muslims are proud to belong to the "Community of the Prophet" and to the "House of Islam," entities which, to them, are synonymous with peace, justice and brotherhood. In their zeal to see the "rights of God" prevail throughout the world, so that the duties and rights of human beings might be respected everywhere, they may use means which are not forbidden by Islam, for example, the giving of alms to "those whose hearts are to be reconciled," and for use in "the cause of Allah" (Qur'an 9:60). That which might be taken for fanaticism is usually the result of an all-encompassing vision, an almost totalitarian understanding of the relationship between religion and state. Today, though, one of the most pressing problems is that of the new relationships between political power and diverse religious communities in most modern nations, where religious and cultural pluralism is the rule.

Perhaps the main objection made against Islam is that it practices "holy war" (a poor translation of the word *jihad*). There is too much confusion among Christians about this subject. The Qur'an has many verses about jihad, dealing with its conduct and its outcome, as well as the manner of dividing its spoils. Later classical Islamic law developed this institution into an international code for warfare, with the intention of regulating the practice of war and reducing its ill effects. In history war and religion were often joined together, unfortunately, whether in the holy wars of the Muslims or the Crusades of the Christians. All historians are agreed today that there is no more place for such practices, that humanity will not put up with violence committed in the name of law and religion. On the contrary many Muslims at the present time seek to follow the teachings of their saints and mystics, speaking of engaging in the "great jihad," as one of the hadith words it. This "great jihad" is a spiritual struggle against all forms of injustice, hate and war, beginning with their predisposing factors in the human heart: selfishness, pride and violence. In quite a few Muslim countries jihad is now identified with the struggle of the whole population against economic and cultural underdevelopment. In this perspective the most appropriate endeavor is the struggle for justice, love and brotherhood, although to carry it out may necessitate a resort to violence occasionally. It is also understood that the "great jihad" is identical with the effort of all people of good will to respect the Universal Declaration of Human Rights and to apply faithfully the measures that are derived from it.

5. Is Islam Opposed to Change?

In the course of the last few centuries Muslim societies have given the impression of being immovable in the scientific, sociological and political fields, and many have thought that Islam itself was primarily responsible for this situation. For some observers the Islamic faith and its philosophical implications make it impossible for Muslims to accept new scientific inventions and to use modern technology. Such critics would consider that Muslims can never be more than consumers in the modern world. Accusations of medieval obscurantism and antipathy to modernity have been made from many non-Muslim quarters.

Once again the Christian partner in dialogue with Muslims must distinguish between theory and practice, between what has happened historically, always imperfect, and the perfect goal that transcends human accomplishment. In fact there is no proof that Islam is incapable of change, contrary to the claims of many. During the Middle Ages Muslims built brilliant civilizations and were at the forefront of scientific research and technological advance. Baghdad, Cordoba and other great cities witnessed a flourishing of medicine, astronomy, mathematics, literature, philosophy and theology. We can, then, see nothing in Islamic faith alone that would be opposed to scientific progress and to metaphysical reflection.

In their attachment to the law revealed by God and to the elaborations of jurisprudence, Muslims have always recognized that they can make certain changes which take account of local customs and situations. This is possible without calling into question the fundamental values of religion, personality, intelligence, family and property. Some innovative practices (*bid'as*) have been rejected in favor of conservatism, but others have been considered as good and integrated into the normative behavior of the community.

Reformers in Islam have always insisted on the distinction between articles of faith (*'aqa'id*), practices of worship (*'ibadat*), ethical norms (*akhlaq*) and social relations (*mu'amalat*). The faith of believers is in-

volved in all of these categories, but in the case of the last two, Muslims are
expected to exercise their conscience and intelligence to work out practical applications and to adapt the norms of jurisprudence to local variations in society. This is certainly a fruitful principle of balanced evolution,
provided that discernment is made in the spirit of faith. The same can be
said for political systems, provided that the basic principle of "consultation" (*shura*) is respected. Thus both parliamentary and revolutionary
systems practice shura, although in different ways. As has been seen, Islamic society is capable of a flexibility and a dynamism that can free it
from the conservatism of former times.

6. Is Islam a Religion of Fear?

Islam is frequently regarded as a religion of fear because its rites of
worship and its emphasis on scrupulous obedience to the Law sometimes
give the impression that God is only "the Majestic, the Compeller, the
Superb" (Qur'an 59:23), "the Absolute" (Qur'an 39:4). It is understand-
able that believers' sense of the divine transcendence and their effort to be
submissive to God tend to emphasize those Most Beautiful Names of God
that would represent him as being awesome and inaccessible, "Able to
requite (the wrong)" (Qur'an 3:4) and "severe in punishment" (Qur'an
2:165). Such emphasis overlooks, however, the continual reference to
God's mercy, forgiveness, kindness and goodness. The Qur'an even says
that God loves His creatures. Nearly forty times it is asserted that "God
loves the pious and the righteous," while "He does not love evildoers."
And, although Muslim mystics describe the first stage of their spiritual
journey as that of "fear" (*khawf*), it should be pointed out that this fear,
servile at first, quickly becomes reverential (*taqwa*), nourished as it is by
trust and hope.

In general, classical Islam, especially the Sunni tendency, has avoided
speaking of a believer's love for God. This is to avoid any suggestion of
direct resemblance between God and His creature, or of an equal exchange between them, developments that would contradict Islam's sense
of the divine transcendence and its refusal to recognize any associate with
God. However, in the course of the centuries it seems that mystical ideas,
popularized by the teachings of religious orders, have influenced Muslims
to give "love, as between friends" (*mahabba*), a more important place in
their thinking about divine-human relationships. This is seen in their
vocabulary, their feelings and their attitudes, so that it is not uncommon
to hear it said that "Islam is a religion of love" (*Al-Islam din mahabba*).

We have already seen that Islam has evolved in a variety of ways that there are many possible interpretations of its way of life. So, we do not have the right to identify the essential nature of that faith with any particular historical manifestations of it. Christians have often done this with regard to the Muslim world, and it has led to prejudices which misrepresent the authentic values of Islam, even when such interpretations are based upon the observed behavior of certain Muslims here and there. All hasty judgments about Islam need to be tempered by rigorous historical, psychological and theological analyses. Only in this way can the Christian mentality be liberated from the errors of judgment and false generalizations which are engendered by prejudice.

III
DISCOVERING THE MUSLIM VIEW
OF CHRISTIANITY

Muslims, whatever their attitude toward dialogue, do not approach Christians without certain predetermined ideas regarding Christianity and the people who profess it. It should not be thought that these ideas are simply personal opinions or prejudices. From the beginning Islam has expressed opinions about Christianity and has developed them through the centuries. Sometimes when Christians hear a Muslim description of Christianity they are quite confused, even shocked, to find that the image given of their faith and practice does not correspond to that which they really believe and practice. It has even happened on some recent occasions that Christians have not even recognized themselves in the description that the Muslims have meant to give of Christianity and its adherents. Nevertheless Muslims feel that Islam has given them in advance an authentic view of Christianity and of Christians, one in which the sole criterion for assessment is the Qur'an.

It is appropriate, then, that Christians be knowledgeable of what Muslims think and say regarding Christian beliefs and practices. In that way the origin of suspicions, misunderstandings and perplexity can be determined. Christians can, by giving an objective and calm explanation of the points at issue, provide Muslims with the opportunity to know them as they are and as they desire to be.

1. The Claim that the Christian Scriptures Have Been Falsified

In dialogue Christians often hear their Muslim friends affirm that they believe in all books that have been revealed by God, that is, the

Torah, the Psalms, the Gospel and the Qur'an, but that they have not read, nor do they seriously consider reading, the first three of these, at least as they exist among Jews and Christians today. This attitude is only to be expected from the Muslims' point of view. On the one hand, the Qur'an tells them to say to the People of Scripture: "We believe in that which hath been revealed unto us and revealed unto you; our God and your God is One, and unto Him we surrender" (Qur'an 29:46). On the other hand, it teaches that "some of those who are Jews change words from their context" (Qur'an 4:46) and "forget a part of that whereof they were admonished" (Qur'an 5:13), so that hearers of the Qur'an are asked, "Have you any hope that they will be true to you when a party of them used to listen to the Word of Allah, then used to change it, after they had understood it, knowingly?" (Qur'an 2:75).

It is for this reason that Islam has said that the Jewish and Christian Scriptures have not been handed down in their original form and have not been passed on according to the divine will. The texts presently in existence have been reworked so that both the letter and the spirit of the message have been changed. It is because of this belief that the Torah and Gospel are accused of having been falsified (*tahrif*). The authentic Torah and Gospel, as originally revealed, and as similar to the Qur'an, the final revelation, simply do not exist, so no one has access to them. This position perhaps explains why the Qur'an does not cite a single verse from the Pentateuch, the Psalms or the Gospels, even though its content shows strong, if not literal, similarity to the canonical and apocryphal biblical traditions.

Christians need to be aware of this point of view which seriously questions the authenticity of their Scriptures and makes the use of the texts in dialogue of questionable value. It is true that Muslim theologians and apologists have employed Jewish and Christian canonical texts in order to find support for a particular Islamic argument. The fact that Moses prophesied the coming of a prophet (the Messiah)[4] and that Jesus promised to send a Paraclete (the Holy Spirit)[5] are, according to Muslim interpretation, additional prophecies of the coming of Muhammad. These exist in a context of Scriptures that have been partially falsified.

Likewise Christians should know about the so-called Gospel of Barnabas[6] that many Muslim scholars consider today to be the only true Gospel. They read it in Arabic translation, although the one ancient manuscript of the text that exists is in Italian and dates from the end of the sixteenth century. Although there are some unanswered questions regarding the origin of the document and the name of its author, it is fairly clear to the impartial reader that the Gospel of Barnabas is apocryphal and of recent composition. It is a spurious Gospel that attempts to prove too much, since in it Jesus affirms that he is not the Messiah and assumes the role of John the Baptist. Muhammad is described as the model for creation and declared to be the awaited Messiah. It also says that Jesus did not die, since Judas was crucified in his place, as a substitute.

At the same time it would be useful for Christians to know that certain ancient and modern Muslim scholars,[7] some of them very eminent, have considered that the falsification of the text (*tahrif al-nass*) is historically impossible, given the large number of manuscripts that exist and the geographical dispersion of the religious communities concerned. Such scholars simply reproach the People of Scripture for having interpreted badly the meaning of their Scriptures (*tahrif al-ma'ani*). While taking account of such observations and of the fact that Muslims and Christians have quite different ways of regarding the revelation, inspiration and canonicity of holy Scriptures, Christians can remind their partners in dialogue that they consider themselves to be "People of a Person," and not "People of Scripture." For them Jesus Christ Himself is the revelation of the Father, that is, of God among humankind, since it is in Him and by Him that the Father communicates with human beings, and through Him that they come to know God fully. The holy Scriptures give Christians access to the revelation of God in Jesus Christ, but only in close linkage with living tradition and within the community of faith (the Church). "Sacred tradition and sacred Scripture form one sacred deposit of the word of God, which is committed to the Church" (*Dei Verbum,* No. 10).

2. The Claim that the Christian Mysteries Are Ineffectual

In Quranic passages regarding Jesus a phrase occurs several times, concluding that "the sects among them [Christians] differ" (Qur'an 19:37). This is seen by some as an echo of the Christological debates which set Nestorians, Monophysites and Melchites against each other in the sixth and seventh centuries. In fact the Quranic statements and denials noted above (Chapter Three) regarding the prophetic role of Jesus should be placed in a context of polemic between Christians, first of all, then between Christians and Jews, and finally between Christians, Jews and Muslims. It would be useless and even harmful to continue such debates in dialogue at the present time in the same way that they were carried on during the Middle Ages. It is not likely that by philosophical reasoning or by theological arguments, no matter how good they may be, Muslims and Christians can arrive at agreement on these subjects.

When Christians speak about the doctrines of the Trinity, the Incarnation and Redemption or even make passing reference to their importance in the life of the Church, they should be sensitive to the thoughts and feelings of Muslims on these subjects. Because of the teachings of their Book, their traditions and their theology, most Muslims understand the Christian Trinity as a subtle attribution of multiplicity to the divine nature. This amounts to saying that God has equals. That is why Ibn Taymiyya accused Christians of "limited polytheism" (*shirk muqayyad*).

These are the facts, and the Qur'an affirms, "It befitteth not (the Majesty of) Allah that He should take unto Himself a son. Glory be to Him!" (Qur'an 19:35). Likewise it is not fitting that God should participate in the life of humanity and pass through the experience of death, even if it be out of love for His creatures and for their highest good. The Muslim reaction is a repeated, "Glory be to Him!" So, Christians should understand this rejection of their mysteries as signifying strict faithfulness on the part of Muslims to their revelation of the impenetrable mystery of God, One and Transcendent. Even though the formulations rejected by the Qur'an are often those of false doctrines held by heterodox Christianity, they have been interpreted by all Muslims in the succeeding centuries as negating the true mysteries professed by Christians.

While recognizing this situation, Christians might request that Muslims show a greater respect for these mysteries that lie at the heart of their life of faith. Christians might point out that these elements of faith are not later theological accretions due to the Hellenistic zeal of an innovating apostle named Paul, but that they are sublime realities, experienced first of all by Jesus and then by every Christian. The belief of Christians is that God the Father revealed Himself in that very Jesus, the eternal Word become flesh among human beings, in order better to reveal to all the mystery of the Father and the grandeur of the human condition, encompassing as it does both suffering and death.

3. The Claim that Christianity Is Not a Pure Monotheism

In the face of this accusation Christians have only to affirm unyieldingly the monotheism that they inherited from Jesus Christ and from the biblical tradition, continually pointing out the manifestations and implications of that belief. "Hear, O Israel: The Lord our God is one Lord" (Deuteronomy 6:4) are the words that Christians have always repeated with Jews everywhere. Then in their creed, they confess: "We believe in ONE God, the Father Almighty . . . and in Jesus Christ, his only Son, our Lord . . . and in the Holy Spirit, the Lord, the giver of life." And many worshipers end their sign of the cross with the insistent word that God is One, and that to him belong "the Kingdom, the power and the glory, for ever and ever."

The divine attribute of unity is central to Christian theology, even as it is to the prayer of Christ and his followers. In 1215 the Fourth Lateran Council declared, in support of the divine unity and counteracting the excesses of Joachim of Fiore: "The divine substance or essence or nature" is that "supreme reality, sublime and unfathomable, who is at one and the same time Father, Son and Holy Spirit, who is the one source of all things, without whom nothing could exist . . . a reality that neither begets nor is begotten." Thus, the mysterious unitary interpersonal relations of Father, Son and Holy Spirit, which are at the heart of Christian faith, remain nevertheless wholly within the Godhead itself. Theology has always stated that the external acts of God proceed from the three Persons "as from one and the same source."

Christians need to call attention to the fact that the mystery of unity is basic to the divine nature, issuing from the unitary fellowship which brings together Father, Son and Holy Spirit. Let them manifest, then, in personal experience, the mystery of their life "hidden in Jesus Christ," by the love of the Father and under the inspiration of the Holy Spirit. Let them talk of this life to others, using words which respect the mystery of divine unity as well as the feelings of the Muslim believer. The words of the Gospel are useful in this regard, helping Christians to express the mystery of their "adoption as children" in simple and concrete terms. Thereby they follow the example of the One who is the perfect Son in His relations with the Father.

4. The Claim that the Church Is Only an Earthly Power

Since Muslims have a keen sense of their belonging to a community (*umma*) of salvation, they can easily appreciate the importance of communal solidarity that Christians experience within the Church. Believers recognize the need for a social setting in which the content of faith is transmitted and its authenticity maintained, and where, through ritual practices and human relationships, certain religious and moral values are inculcated. Each community has its particular rites of admission, its official places of worship and its corps of religious specialists. In this regard Muslims have regarded with admiration the organizational structure of the

Catholic Church and the efficiency with which Christians perform services in schools, hospitals and social work. Some of them take an interest in the declarations (encyclicals, pastoral letters) and actions (peace initiatives) of the Holy See, appreciating their moral influence and believing that they represent the official Christian point of view. They also are quite aware of the activities of the World Council of Churches.

Nevertheless Muslims find it difficult to understand the distinctions made by Christians today between Church, Christianity and Christendom. Their particular view of the close ties between temporal and spiritual powers leads them to consider traditionally Christian countries as Christian states, and the Church as the religious expression of the power that governs them. Some Muslims look for a Christian policy in such states, at least in its general lines, even as could be found in the Christendom of former times. Such an expectation explains why they so easily accuse Christians of being passive in the face of the injustices of the colonial era, and of colluding with the Western powers at the time of the Church's missionary expansion. Many negative statements made about Islam by Christians of former times are apt to be understood by Muslims as being the official position of the Church instead of seeing them in the light of politico-cultural conflicts and the prejudices and the ignorance of those times. Many Muslims believe that the Church should intervene more often and more directly in the affairs of traditionally Christian countries, in order to "enjoin what is right and forbid evil."

From their faith perspectives of both similarity and divergence Christians and Muslims would do well to think together on the particular role that religion should play in the building of human society, taking into account the risk of intolerance when a state is founded on specifically religious principles. History records many sad examples in this regard. The partners in dialogue might well ask themselves such important questions as: What principles do Muslims envisage for the pluralistic societies in which they live today? How do Christians intend to transform their noble ideals into practical action? By giving serious attention to these questions Christians will make known what is, to them, the mystery of the Church, "sacrament of the continued presence of Christ" and primary sign of the coming Kingdom of God.

5. The Claim that Christians Have Been Unfaithful to the Message of Jesus

Muslims always admire Christians who sincerely try to practice the ideals of the Gospel in their lives. In this regard, the Qur'an speaks of the beneficial example of monks within the Church: "We . . . placed compassion and mercy in the hearts of those who followed him [Jesus]. But monasticism they invented—We ordained it not for them—only seeking Allah's pleasure, and they observed it not with right observance" (Qur'an 57:27). The Christian ideal is clearly stated here, but the text says that rare are those who put it into practice. The Qur'an adds: "We gave those of them who believe their reward, but many of them are evil-livers" (Qur'an 57:27).

These verses show why Muslims have two contrasting attitudes toward their Christian partners in dialogue: on the one hand some are inwardly attracted to and fascinated by the message of the Beatitudes as lived by Jesus, whereas others are either silently or openly critical of the imperfect way Christians have followed Jesus' message of love and of those ascetic and mystical practices that are deemed excessive. History justifies both attitudes, for although many Christians have failed to carry out the requirements of the Gospel, there has been a long succession of mystics and saints who have followed Jesus closely in a most admirable way. Realizing that these two contrasting attitudes exist, Christians note that whereas, according to the Qur'an, they were intended to be "helpers of God" (Qur'an 3:52) and defenders of Christ, Muslims have found them to have "exaggerated" (Qur'an 4:171) in their doctrines, to have gone astray in their daily life and to have yielded to the authority of priests and monks who claim to have the power of mediation, thus standing in the way of direct contact between a believer and God.

Since Christians make "exaggerated" claims about Jesus Christ, believe in irrational mysteries and say, "We are the sons of Allah and His loved ones" (Qur'an 5:18), provoking the Quranic retort, "Why then doth He chastise you for your sins?" (Qur'an 5:18), it is perhaps natural for many Muslims to think that through history Christianity has deviated from its origins. To them it seems that at the beginning the Christian religion conformed to the image reflected by the Qur'an of an early Judeo-Christianity. This is why many Muslims believe that Christians will be condemned to the "Abode of Punishment." However, certain ancient and modern scholars in Islam have judged that all non-Muslims of good faith will have access to the "Abode of Reward."[8]

It is evident that Muslims find it difficult to accept the Christianity of today as authentic and to believe in the complete sincerity of those who practice it. History seems to corroborate their doubts. The only way they can be freed of such feelings is to see Christians who practice truly the ways of the Gospel, in obedience to the message of Jesus. To the degree that witnesses of the Gospel are open in spirit and not exclusive there will be progress toward understanding and mutual acceptance.

IV
OBSTACLES THAT REMAIN

Even if Muslims and Christians should agree to forget the wrongs of the past, trying to free themselves of prejudice and paying attention to the way each group regards the other, there would still remain certain practical difficulties in the way of coming together in mutual understanding. It would be illusory and vain to ignore these in an effort to practice dialogue. Both Muslims and Christians know from experience that these obstacles have to do with customs, regulations and conditions which carry much weight, whose influence is difficult to avoid. They should be honest and open enough to discuss these freely and objectively so that neither party can be accused of ulterior motives or of using dialogue for its own ends.

1. Dietary Restrictions

In their life together, including eating and drinking, Christians and Muslims often are faced with the problem of dietary restrictions. These can cause a hindrance even to the most straightforward and friendly relationships. It should be remembered that Muslims are forbidden to eat "Carrion and blood and swine-flesh, and that which hath been dedicated unto any other than Allah, and the strangled, and the dead" whose blood has not been drained (Qur'an 5:3). The Qur'an says that "strong drink and games of chance . . . are only an infamy of Satan's handiwork. Leave it aside, in order that ye may succeed" (Qur'an 5:90). Christians should be aware of the dietary requirements of their Muslim friends so that when they prepare meals and refreshments members of both religious communities will feel at ease, the Muslims in faithfulness to the prescriptions of their religion and the Christians in the joyous freedom of Christ's followers, whose Master came to declare all foods lawful, since evil is what "proceeds from the heart" to "defile a man" (Matthew 15:18–20). Each party is then free to act according to its conscience, and each respects the choice of the other.

2. Mixed Marriages

The frequent movement and intermingling of peoples across the earth at this time has resulted almost everywhere in mixed marriages. Many partners in these unions try to use their difference in religion as a means for drawing closer together in dialogue. Although some of the marriages between Muslims and Christians have succeeded and others have failed, their consequences are usually difficult, even unhappy, for the partners and especially for the children. This is why the two religious communities have always tried rightfully to discourage such marriages by creating legal obstructions. In its rulings the Church makes no difference between man and woman. Islam, on the contrary, permits a Muslim man to marry a Christian woman but prohibits a Muslim woman from marrying a Christian man. In addition, when a Muslim man marries a Christian woman the difficulties encountered by the latter to obtain custody (*hadana*) of the children in case of the breakup of the marriage, and the limitations upon her right to inherit property because of her different religion (*ikhtilaf al-din*), often cause misunderstandings which may lead to bitterness and animosity. Partners in dialogue need to learn carefully the various regulations which, when in conflict with each other, too often result in family crises. There is a tendency to judge too hastily that the respective religions are solely responsible for the difficult situations. Indeed the success of these Islamo-Christian unions depends upon how carefully those involved are informed of the implications of their situation. Such marriages can and should be extraordinarily favorable environments for dialogue.

3. The Duty of the Apostolate

We have described elsewhere how the apostolate, involving the full commitment of believers, should be understood as a completely unselfish witness, having as its sole intention a sharing of the gifts of God with others. However, actual practices are sometimes in strange contrast with the ideal that is agreed upon in dialogue. Christians and Muslims must both expect to be accused of inappropriate proselytism. They should be ready to justify the methods, means and goals of their apostolate. They must discuss this question at still greater length in their times of formal dialogue. Of course all believers are required to be true to their faith and to their community. This is an essential value recognized equally by both Islam and Christianity, a value that the two religions have sometimes sought to safeguard by the use of certain laws. Although both recognize that there should never be any coercion in matters of religion, Christians must remember that Islamic law forbids Muslims to give up their religion for another (*ridda*), and it prescribes severe punishment for such a transgression. It seems that at present Muslim societies find it rather difficult to accept the principle of religious liberty that grants to each adult person the right to adopt the religion of his or her choice.[9] This fact can be the source of serious mutual misunderstandings.

4. The Problem of Religious Minorities

On the difficult question of religious minorities Muslims and Christians tend often to encounter mutual incomprehension. One reason for this is the difficulty that both the majority and the minority groups experience in trying to achieve a balance in a pluralistic society. Also the differing views held by one and the other regarding the relationship of religion and state pose an obstacle to understanding. Christians have difficulty grasping the demands of Muslim minorities for religious autonomy when such a status is held to include the cultural, legal and even political aspects of life. For their part Muslims are surprised to learn that their Christian compatriots refuse to accept the "status of protected citizen" (*dhimma*) as maintained in the classical Islamic society,[10] and demand to be considered as full citizens in modern society, even as they are so recognized by the constitutions of many countries. Dialogue is essential on this subject so that the parties concerned might reach some compromise in the interest of a well-ordered pluralistic society. In that way the needs of minority communities would be provided for in countries where the institutions and legal systems were set up originally for homogeneous populations. This process has been carried out in a number of Asian and African nations. There remains the danger, however, of deep misunderstanding between the Muslim and the Christian points of view.

These are, then, four points on which there seems to be flagrant disagreement between Muslims and Christians. Fortunately there are many believers who are able to see these obstacles to interreligious harmony in their true perspective. Of course they hope to eliminate them eventually, but there are many factors beyond their control which stand in the way of this. In the meantime such elements of disharmony must be taken into account as efforts are continued to bring about mutual reconciliation.

Notes

1. See the Bibliography, especially N.A. Daniel, *Islam and the West,* and R.W. Southern, *Western Views of Islam.*
2. This whole question was treated by Jacques Lanfry at the Seminar for Muslim-Christian Dialogue in Tripoli, Libya, February 1976: "What must we do to combat the prejudices and misunderstandings that separate us?" Mimeographed document, in *Current Documenta-*

tion, No. 5, April 1976. Published by the White Fathers' Documentation Office in Rome. A partial translation of the original French text appeared in *Journal of Ecumenical Studies* 14 (1977), pp. 484–500.

3. See Bibliography, especially J.N.D. Anderson, *Islamic Law in the Modern World,* New York and London, 1959; and, in addition, Maurice Borrmans, *Statut Personnel et Famille au Maghreb de 1940 à nos jours,* Paris and La Haye, Mouton, 1977, and *Documents sur la famille au Maghreb de 1940 à nos jours (avec les textes législatifs marocain, algérien, tunisien et égyptien en matière de Statut Personnel musulman),* Rome, Istituto per l'Oriente, 1979.

4. Deuteronomy 18:15 and 18:18–19.

5. John 14:15–17; 14:26; 15:26; 16:7–8; 16:13–14.

6. A photocopy of the Italian text of the manuscript has been published, with introduction, French translation and notes, by L. Cirillo and M. Frémaux, *Evangile de Barnabé, Recherches sur la composition et l'origine. Texte en traduction,* Paris: Beauchesne, 1977. See also J. Jomier, "L'Evangile selon Barnabé," *MIDEO* (Cairo), No. 6 (1959–1961), 137–226; Jan Slomp, "The Gospel in Dispute," *Islamochristiana* (Rome), No. 4 (1978), 67–112; and Mikel De Epalza, "Le milieu hispano-mauresque de l'Evangile islamisant de Barnabé (XVIe–XVIIe s.)," *Islamochristiana* (Rome), No. 8 (1982), 185–200.

7. Among others mention can be made of a hadith from Al-Darimi (798–869), the *Risala adhawiyya fi l-ma'ad* of Ibn Sina (980–1037), the polemical work *Al-Radd al-Jamil* of Al-Ghazali (1059–1111), the Qur'an commentary (*Tafsir*) of Razi (1149–1209), the *Muqaddima* of Ibn Khaldun (1332–1402), the text of *Al-Dhikr al-Hakim* of Kamil Husayn (1901–1977), the opinions of Sayyid Khan (1817–1898), and the position of Muhammad 'Abduh (1849–1905) in his Qur'an commentary (*Tafsir*) of *Al-Manar.*

8. Such as the Brethren of Purity (*Ikhwan al-Safa'*) (tenth century), al-Ghazali, Muhammad 'Abduh, Dr. Kamil Husayn; see "L' Islam et les religions non musulmanes: Quelques textes positifs," *Islamochristiana* (Rome) 3 (1977), 39–63.

9. The Universal Declaration of Human Rights declares in Article 18 that "every person has the right to freedom of thought, of conscience and religion; this right implies the freedom to change religion or conviction, as well as the freedom to make public one's religion or conviction, alone or in community, in public as in private, by teaching, practice, worship and ritual."

10. On this question see A. Fattal, *Le statut légal des non-musulmans en pays d'Islam,* Beirut, 1958.

Chapter Five
Areas of Cooperation

Today the human race is passing through "a true social and cultural transformation, one which has repercussions on man's religious life as well" (*Gaudium et Spes,* No. 4). People are bewildered by the alarming contradictions which they both cause and endure in modern life. They see wealth and poverty, affluence and misery, power and weakness, boldness and resignation, freedom and subjugation, knowledge and ignorance, technological progress and underdevelopment, health and sickness, life and death. These are some of the more flagrant imbalances that afflict the modern world and that distort all relationships between nations, communities and individuals.

All believers of Islam, Christianity and Judaism should join people of good will of whatever religion or ideology to furnish concrete responses, including a common message and coordinated action, to the human situation. The fundamental problems are the same for all communities, and believers must provide solutions, both by act and by word, as their faith in God and their love for humanity guide them. "What is man? What is this sense of sorrow, of evil, of death, which continues to exist despite so much progress? What is the purpose of these victories, purchased at so high a cost? What can man offer to society, what can he expect from it? What follows this earthly life?" (*Gaudium et Spes,* No. 10).

I
THE FULFILLMENT OF CREATION

Those of monotheistic faith, such as Muslims, Jews and Christians, believe that the world is the result, not of chance or of necessity, but of a marvelous plan of which only God knows the secret, since he is both the initiator of it and the one who will bring it to completion. Believers especially, then, should do what they can to help the world to prosper and to progress toward perfect conformity to that for which God created it. They are called to this by God, who in his sovereign love has chosen to enlist the cooperation of human beings. As a sign of this noble calling humanity reflects in miniature, as it were, both the magnitude of the world and its minuteness. Christians know that "the creation waits with eager longing for the revealing of the sons of God; for the creation was subjected to futility, not of its own will but by the will of him who subjected it in hope; because the creation itself will be set free from its bondage to decay and obtain the glorious liberty of the children of God. We know that the whole creation has been groaning in travail together until now" (Romans 8:19–22). And from their side, Muslims remember that God "hath made serviceable unto you whatsoever is in the skies and whatsoever is in the earth" (Qur'an 31:20), and, further, God "hath made of service unto you the rivers; and maketh the sun and the moon, constant in their courses, to be of service unto you, and hath made of service unto you the night and the day. And He giveth you of all ye ask of Him" (Qur'an 14:32–34). So it is in the name of God, whose creation of delicate and vital balance foreshadows a higher universal harmony, that believers are called upon to play an effective role in the eventual consummation of the world. It is by participating in this "completion of creation" that all prepare for the revelation of "a new heaven and a new earth" (Revelation 21:1).

A new quest is needed for relationships of respect, obedience and flexibility between humankind and nature, to replace those of pollution, violence and subjection. These would in turn lead to new relationships between technology and nature, so that the irreversible processes of urbanization, industrialization and mass consumption might be tempered by a control over human appetites and a respect for nature, from whence come the material benefits of the earth. Is it necessarily utopian to imagine that technology might adopt a human face and learn to unite what is beautiful with that which is true and good? Art and culture have always had something to say in the fulfillment of creation, and all civilizations, however primitive, have demonstrated this. God in His wisdom challenges men and women of faith to act responsibly in this respect, so that their influence in the world will reflect the ideals of brotherhood which they seek to see exemplified in society.

II
SERVICE TO HUMANKIND

"According to the almost unanimous opinion of believers and unbelievers alike, all things on earth should be related to man as their center and crown" (*Gaudium et Spes,* No. 12). Christians and Muslims affirm the eminent dignity of humanity. This is what constrains them to respect all human beings, defend their rights and render them service.

1. What Is the Origin of Human Dignity?

According to the Islamic view human beings possess an exceptional quality within the created world. The Qur'an affirms that God "formed them (human beings) harmoniously" and breathed into them of his spirit (Qur'an 15:29, rendition by translator), making them his "viceroy (*khalifa*) in the earth," even though they would "do harm therein and . . . shed blood" (Qur'an 2:30). A "trust" (*amana*) was committed to them, a responsibility from which "the heavens and the earth and the hills" turned away (Qur'an 33:72). So, it is said that humans have been "challenged" (*mukhatab*), made responsible (*mukallaf*) by God for all things. This is no doubt why in the Qur'an it is said that the angels bowed down before Adam. There is a prophetic hadith that says, "God created Adam in His image."[1]

For its part, the Christian tradition has developed to a high degree the biblical teaching that "man was created 'to the image of God,' is capable of knowing and loving his Creator, and was appointed by Him as master of all earthly creatures that he might subdue them and use them to God's glory" (*Gaudium et Spes*, No. 12). Subsequently Jesus Christ revealed to men and women the extraordinary dignity that they have in being children adopted by the Father in the name and image of the one who is for all time the Perfect Son. "The Christian man, conformed to the likeness of that Son who is the firstborn of many brothers, receives 'the first-fruits of the Spirit' (Romans 8:23) by which he becomes capable of discharging the new law of love," since "Christ has risen . . . He has lavished life upon us so that, as sons in the Son, we can cry out in the Spirit: Abba, Father!" (*Gaudium et Spes*, No. 22).

Because all human beings share in that high dignity, either in reality or in hope, they have the right to be respected, served and loved. Christians and Muslims are obliged, then, to render service to all people, both collectively and individually, according to their particular needs, since "man . . . is the only creature on earth which God willed for itself" (*Gaudium et Spes*, No. 24). Such is the human being whom all believers are called upon to serve, "man as 'willed' by God, as 'chosen' by him from eternity and called, destined for grace and glory—this is 'each' man, 'the most concrete' man, 'the most real'; this is man in all the fullness of the mystery in which he has become a sharer in Jesus Christ, the mystery in which each one of the four thousand million human beings living on our planet has become a sharer from the moment he is conceived beneath the heart of his mother" (*Redemptor Hominis*, No. 13).

2. How Human Dignity May Best Be Promoted

First of all there is the *dignity of life,* demonstrated by the respect shown to motherhood and the rejection of abortion, by a balanced view of the bodily desires with recognition of their spiritual significance, by the meticulous care taken in treating the sick with absolute respect for the biological functions of their bodies, by persistent efforts to rehabilitate or treat the physically and mentally handicapped, by the warm and intelligent support given to the dying and the courageous refusal of all forms of euthanasia.

Another aspect of human nobility is the *dignity of the spirit.* "Man judges rightly that by his intellect he surpasses the material universe, for he shares in the light of the divine mind" (*Gaudium et Spes,* No. 15). Thus human beings are capable of grasping empirical truths, discovering spiritual realities and exercising wisdom. Respect for the dignity of human intelligence calls for the provision of adequate means for universal education in order that everyone might have access to all forms of culture. Believers judge that such provision results from the action of the Spirit of God. Modern pluralistic societies and the framework of international cultural exchanges provide unusual opportunities for cooperation in intellectual development.

Likewise human grandeur is expressed in the *dignity of the conscience,* understood both psychologically and morally. That is why believers strive to ensure that as material and technical progress takes place it is accompanied by moral and spiritual development. Is the life of modern human beings serving more and more to enhance the dignity of human personality? Are the demands of the conscience becoming clearer, nobler and higher, or are we witnessing a moral regression under the influence of new technology and unbridled mass consumption? Religious faith enables us to emphasize the objective norms of morality that are ultimately grounded in the loving good will of God toward humankind and the world. We can affirm the right of every conscience, even if misguided, to be respected, then enlightened and brought to true freedom.

The mystery of the human conscience leads, then, to the *dignity of freedom.* "This freedom means that all men are to be immune from coercion on the part of individuals or of social groups and of any human power, in such wise that in matters religious no one is to be forced to act in a manner contrary to his own beliefs. Nor is anyone to be restrained from acting in accordance with his own beliefs, whether privately or publicly, whether alone or in association with others, within due limits" (*Dignitatis*

Humanae, No. 2). Believers know by experience that the wise exercise of freedom requires appropriate education along with certain sociological and legal safeguards. So there ought to be a concerted effort to make possible such education and safeguards in any situation where freedom is threatened.

Within their respective national societies and by means of international organizations, believers can manifest their will to cooperate in humanitarian service, without regard to religious or ideological affiliation. Organizations such as the UNO, the UNESCO, the FAO, the BIT, the OMS, the UNICEF, etc., should be able to count on the active support of all men and women of faith, so that the inalienable rights of humankind might be protected throughout the world. In addition Christians and Muslims have developed particular programs of aid, showing their impartial good will to help those in need. Quite a few Christian and humanitarian groups have been joined by Muslims who desire to do their part in the works of social welfare, relief and education that have been undertaken. Of course both parties in such cooperation need to respect each other's particular religious motivations, but together they can, through serving others, advance their dialogue regarding the spiritual values which already unite them, and share together the sublime vision of human grandeur that inspires them.

3. Who Is Most Deserving of Service?

It is by service to the most deprived that believers can best testify to their respect for human dignity. The faith that motivates their acts is most clearly seen in the zeal with which they seek to help and deliver the oppressed (*mustad'afun*) from their burdens, comfort and teach the orphans and the handicapped, and treat the lepers and mentally ill. The true extent of their love for humanity is proven by the degree to which they show kindness for the marginalized of society, affection for the elderly, and tenderness toward the dying. Even atheists are not excluded from this human concern, for their dignity is fully recognized, even though their denial of God involves certain serious possibilities for undermining human dignity and for disturbing the peace of the world. By suggesting to atheists that every person is a "path toward God" believers may best be able to show that humanity is "a reflection of God, the highest manifestation of visible creation," rendering glory to the One who formed it.

Christians and Muslims should cooperate in showing basic respect and a helpful spirit toward the masses of those in whose favor the Beatitudes speak: "Blessed are the poor in spirit, for theirs is the kingdom of heaven. Blessed are those who mourn, for they shall be comforted. Blessed are the meek, for they shall inherit the earth. Blessed are those who hunger and thirst for righteousness, for they shall be satisfied. Blessed are the merciful, for they shall obtain mercy. Blessed are the pure in heart, for they shall see God. Blessed are the peacemakers, for they shall be called sons of God. Blessed are those who are persecuted for righteousness' sake, for theirs is the kingdom of heaven" (Matthew 5:1–10). For their part, Muslims are ever mindful that the Qur'an requires that they put into practice their own ideals of justice and mercy: "And serve Allah. Ascribe nothing as partner unto Him. (Show) kindness unto parents, and unto near kindred, and orphans, and the needy, and unto the neighbour who is not of kin, and the fellow-traveller and the wayfarer and (the slaves) whom your right hands possess" (4:36). All those, then, who go back to Abraham in their religious traditions can together join with all who hold to the Universal Declaration of Human Rights, calling attention to the fact that the people who should be given first priority in the defense of those rights are the ones who have been long deprived of them and whose cries of distress continually rise to God.

III
THE ORGANIZATION OF SOCIETY

Human dignity in all of its aspects can only be assured in an inclusive society where the values that promote that dignity are honored. Believers have always sought to build a society of brotherhood in which the conflicts that plague humanity are finally resolved. In former times Muslims spoke ideally of the "excellent city" (*al-madina al-fadila*), and they still hope to establish an earthly society in which the laws of God prevail. However, they are not at all agreed on the methods, the stages and the limits of what they undertake. Christians say, "The shape of this world will pass away . . . God is preparing a new dwelling place and a new earth where justice will abide, and whose blessedness will answer and surpass all the longings for peace which spring up in the human heart" (*Gaudium et Spes*, No. 39). But this "expectation of a new earth" should awaken in all hearts the desire to develop in the present time "a new human family, a body which even now is able to give some kind of foreshadowing of the new age" as it contributes "to the better ordering of human society" (*Gaudium et Spes*, No. 39). Within the pluralistic framework of this human family Christians and Muslims can work together, since the latter hear from their Scripture, "We have made you nations and tribes that ye may know one another" (Qur'an 49:13).

Along the same lines everyone realizes that "profound and rapid changes make it particularly urgent that no one, ignoring the trend of events or drugged by laziness, content himself with a merely individualistic morality" (*Gaudium et Spes,* No. 30). It is to be hoped that people will consent "to the unavoidable requirements of social life," and take on "the manifold demands of human partnership. . . . The will to play one's role in common endeavors should be everywhere encouraged," as well as participation "in public affairs" (*Gaudium et Spes,* No. 31). By emphasizing the ideal of responsible participation Christians and Muslims can recommend to their contemporaries a form of cooperation that gives first priority to human solidarity and respects all legitimate means for expressing it. Members of the two religions have certain urgent problems to work out among themselves that affect the quality of life in their communities: marriage and the family, culture, economic and social life, politics, the unity of peoples and peace between nations.

1. The Dignity of Marriage and the Family

Believers can help to solve the difficult problems faced by families in these times, while at the same time respecting the regional traditions that might prevail, taking into account the nature of the family in a particular culture, whether it be patriarchal or strictly conjugal. Some of the issues are: freedom to choose one's marriage partner, financial independence for new families, adequate housing, the responsibility of the wife, the rights of children, responsible fatherhood and motherhood, conjugal harmony, presence of the elderly in the home, relations between the generations. Believers desirous of being of service to their societies should share together their experiences and their aspirations with regard to family life. Often Muslims are gratified to find that their Christian friends have the same ideals as theirs for marriage and the family. Both purpose to give an example of "the authentic dignity of persons . . . joined to one another in equal affection," thus manifesting the eminent quality of marriage to ennoble both love and life.

A further possible common action for believers is to promote the high dignity of human sexuality by denouncing cheap pleasure-seeking and vulgar forms of eroticism, by affirming full respect for human life in opposition to abortion and infanticide as "unspeakable crimes" (*Gaudium et Spes,* No. 51). There are in fact many opportunities where witness can be borne to these high ideals of marriage and the family: sexual education for adolescents, preparation of engaged couples for marriage, maternity and child care centers, social services for those couples who become separated, family and educational groups, and many other occasions for promoting the values of love and life by the concerted action especially of those who are competent in biology, medicine, psychology and the social sciences. The partners in mixed marriages have a role to play in this area when they cultivate together those ideals of marriage and the family that their two religious traditions have in common. When a couple, a Christian and a Muslim, work out in a constructive way all of the aspects of their conjugal relationship they become both witnesses and precursors of a common action by Christians and Muslims in behalf of married couples and families.

2. Development of the Arts and Culture

Believers are faced with the task of helping to create a new balance between the cultural traditions of the past, which are particular to each region of the world, and the uniform culture engendered by modern technological and international civilization. Combining a respect for the past with a sensitivity to present realities, they can work for a culture that exhibits the interaction of humanistic and technical values. People should be faced with their "right to culture" and their duty, not only to develop themselves culturally, but also to help others so to develop. Thus the gifts of God will be fulfilled in society. Still another and difficult task is to strive for a "synthesis . . . of the various branches of knowledge and the arts" and a consequent harmony between such a synthesis and the quest of faith by humanity in both its intellectual and its artistic aspects.

In this regard the following statement from Vatican Council II can be seen to be pertinent: "May the faithful, therefore, live in very close union with the men of their time. Let them strive to understand perfectly their way of thinking and feeling, as expressed in their culture. Let them blend modern science and its theories and the understanding of the most recent discoveries with . . . morality and doctrine [according to their particular religious tradition]. Thus their religious practice and morality can keep pace with their scientific knowledge and with an ever-advancing technology" (*Gaudium et Spes,* No. 62).

3. Economic and Social Justice

By virtue of their faith in the living God who is both "generous bestower" and "just providence," believers should show by their deeds that "God intended the earth and all that it contains for the use of every human being and people. Thus, as all men follow justice and unite in charity, created goods should abound for them on a reasonable basis" (*Gaudium et Spes,* No. 69). To do this it must ever be remembered that "man is the source, the center, and the purpose of all socio-economic life" (*Gaudium et Spes,* No. 63).

In their common concern to find solutions to economic and social conflicts, both on the national and on the international levels, they must affirm that economic development is intended to be for the benefit of humanity, always under the control of human beings. "Growth must not be allowed merely to follow a kind of automatic course resulting from the economic activity of individuals. Nor must it be entrusted solely to the authority of government" (*Gaudium et Spes,* No. 65). By insisting on this principle believers can show that there is an alternative way to the inexorable and pitiless grip of capitalism and of collectivism in their excessive forms. New social formulas must be elaborated by concerted action in which concrete regional situations are taken into account as well as local working conditions, in which natural resources are more equitably distributed and the role of highly developed economic powers is precisely defined in balance with the developing economies. The Encyclical of Paul VI, *Populorum Progressio,* already in 1967 set forth what might be the common project of believers and all people of good will to make economic life serve the "integral development of humankind."

4. Political Harmony

The social virtues extolled alike by the different religions encourage believers to inculcate among their people a spirit of civic responsibility that is concerned for the common good of all and for the full protection of human rights. Such a spirit is expressed by assuming concrete responsibilities, such as democratic participation in the management of public affairs, including maintaining the needful autonomy of the legislative, executive and judicial branches of government and defending basic civil liberties. These latter include "the rights of free assembly, of common action, of expressing personal opinions, and of professing a religion both privately and publicly . . . the rights of national minorities . . . while at the same time these minorities honor their duties toward the political community" (*Gaudium et Spes,* No. 73).

Believers are called upon to give an "example of devotion to the sense of duty and of service to the advancement of the common good. Thus they can also show in practice how authority is to be harmonized with freedom, personal initiative with consideration for the bonds uniting the whole social body, and necessary unity with beneficial diversity. . . . Prudently and honorably let them fight against injustice and oppression, the arbitrary rule of one man or one party, and lack of tolerance. Let them devote themselves to the welfare of all sincerely and fairly, indeed with charity and political courage" (*Gaudium et Spes,* No. 75).

5. The Community of Nations and International Peace

In their concern for justice, equality and brotherhood believers cannot limit their vision to the particular national group of which they are a part. The religious message that they proclaim requires them to seek peace on an international scale and ultimately to work for a community of nations. The experience of history and the inspiration of God have taught them that peace is not simply the absence of war, nor is it merely a balance of terror and suspicion. Rather peace is "an enterprise of justice" (Isaiah 32:17) that requires respect for the welfare of all people and that "cannot be obtained . . . unless personal values are safeguarded and men freely and trustingly share with one another the riches of their inner spirits and their talents" (*Gaudium et Spes,* No. 78).

So, all are called to work for peace and reconciliation wherever and whenever possible. They must never forget the inhumanity of all wars, especially that of "total war" and of terrorism. They must denounce all forms of ethnic or cultural genocide, as well as the continual arms race, for "while extravagant sums are being spent on the furnishing of ever new weapons, an adequate remedy cannot be provided for the multiple miseries afflicting the whole modern world" (*Gaudium et Spes,* No. 81). In sum, they must help their fellow human beings to be liberated from their age-old bondage to war by finding ways to settle their differences in a truly human manner.

IV
HUMAN IMITATION OF DIVINE ACTION

The basic human cooperation described above constitutes the permanent setting for dialogue between believers as they are involved side by side with all persons of good will, even with those who are without faith. Whether it involves worldwide development, service to fellow human beings or the organization of society, partners in dialogue have a great deal to say and to do together. As important representatives of the total human experience, they all need to be a permanent part of such cooperation.

Their motivation for such an involvement in service to humanity is of course their faith in God and their sense of closeness to him. By their action in society believers manifest in part their true identity to others, since what they do is intimately linked with the very action of God in the world.

Christians are challenged by the high ideal set for them by Jesus Christ: "Love your enemies and pray for those who persecute you, so that you may be sons of your Father who is in heaven; for he makes his sun rise on the evil and on the good, and sends rain on the just and on the unjust. . . . You, therefore, must be perfect, as your heavenly Father is perfect" (Matthew 5:44–45, 48). And Muslims are told, according to the words of Al-Ghazali: "Clothe yourselves in the ways of God. For believers, perfection lies in a relationship with God wherein His most praiseworthy attributes are taken on, such as knowledge, justice, goodness, kindness, beneficience, mercy, good counsel, encouragement to do good and protection from all evil."[2] Thus by their deeds Muslims arrive at what may be called "an exchange of attributes," something described in a beautiful "divine hadith" (*hadith qudsi*): "The closer my servants draw to me through voluntary good deeds, the more I love them, says God. And when I love them I am the ear with which they hear, the eye with which they see and the tongue with which they speak."

Thus by their joint action Christians and Muslims have the opportunity to render a fresh witness to the reality of God Himself, showing to all that in the midst of the human struggle for fulfillment there is possible an orientation toward the divine mystery. When believers "vie with one another in good works" by serving young people, children, the handicapped, and the sick and dying, by denouncing war and all murderous experimentation, they do so because they consider life to be a gift of God and because they believe in the living God who loves life and who desires to see life come to full fruition. When they struggle against all forms of discrimination (sexual, racial, cultural, religious or national) and against the selfish appropriation of natural resources by individuals or collectivities so as to guarantee justice and equality of opportunity for everyone, they do so because they regard the riches of the earth as gifts from God and because they believe in a just and generous God who creates with largesse and gives without measure.

When believers seek to defend freedom in all its aspects so that humans will recognize and accept their personal responsibility before their own conscience, before their fellow human beings and before God, they do so because, to them, freedom is a gift of God, and because they believe in a God who is free "to do what He wills" in love for all humankind and in view of eliciting their free response to Him. When believers promote dialogue as a means of resolving conflicts and when they work to build a more harmonious and inclusive society, both regionally and internationally, they do so because, to them, peace and unity within diversity are gifts of God, and because they believe in a merciful and compassionate God who forgives and unites, who never despairs even of the people who are the most resistant to His will. Therefore, the concerted action of Christians and Muslims makes it possible for them to give united witness today to the unique value of this world, to the true dignity of human beings, and to the eminent greatness of God. And, further, their specific cooperation in these various types of essential societal endeavor may be considered as a kind of human imitation of God's working, and as at least a partial revelation to the world of the divine activity.

Notes

1. Many Islamic scholars interpret this text as meaning that God created Adam according to the image that He had previously conceived Him to have. Others, such as Al-Ghazali, think that Adam was made to resemble God Himself, and that it is because of this particularity that God chose him as His "viceroy" on the earth.

2. Abu Hamid al-Ghazali, *Ihya' 'ulum al-din (The Revival of Religious Sciences)*, Cairo: Al-Babi al-Halabi, 1358/1939, vol. 4, p. 298. This question is treated by Al-Ghazali under what he calls the fifth cause of love for God, that is, "resemblance, or conformity, since that which is similar to something else is attracted to it, and is more inclined to take on the very form of the object of attraction."

Chapter Six
Potential Areas of Religious Agreement

A dialogue centered in the sharing of ideals and values will not be enough for believers, who know that the basic dialogue is the one which God Himself initiates, develops and fulfills with each person in the framework of his or her religious tradition with its particular possibilities and constraints. They all know that it is the same God with whom they have to do, even though He is understood differently by various ones. They are convinced that God speaks to humankind in history, even if the ways in which He speaks are different for some and for others. In the same way that Christians and Muslims have found much common ground in the ideals and values that motivate their action in service to humanity, they discover the possibilities of speaking to one another about their religious experience as such, their personal responses to the divine initiatives toward humankind, and, more broadly, the rich traditions of piety that have developed through history in both Islam and in Christianity.

If the partners in dialogue are spiritually open to each other they will recognize with joyful gratitude the faithfulness in prayer, the generosity, the fervent practice of religious duties, the love for contemplation and all other manifestations of piety seen in others, even if they belong to different religious traditions. Under such circumstances those in dialogue go beyond a mere intellectual satisfaction in discerning the multiform action of God throughout history. Their hearts are touched by the living example of people who obviously are living under the guidance of God. It is important to discern this divine action in other religions and in their high spiritual achievements not as a scholarly historian of religions or as a scientific "archeologist of spirituality," but rather as a seeker after God, as one eager to assimilate the insights of others, and thereby, in some way, contribute to the praise of the universe for its Creator. Thus believers are enabled to "enlarge the place of their tent" in order to show therein the "very hospitality of Abraham," enabling Christians and Muslims to discover together potential areas of agreement between their respective religious experiences.

Such a spiritual attitude requires that believers be ready to go beyond the sociological limits set by their tradition and environment. In fact when dialogue takes place on the level of vital spiritual life that is ever renewed by deep spiritual experiences, the partners give up an "inert spirituality" which binds them to inherited certitudes and irrelevant values. In its place they adopt a "dynamic spirituality," by which those same certitudes and values become the point of departure for an enthusiastic quest to understand the Word of God in terms of the broad range of human experience. Recently Pope John Paul II reminded Christians that "the Fathers of the Church rightly saw in the various religions as it were so many reflections of the one truth, 'seeds of the Word,' attesting that, though the routes taken may be different, there is but a single goal to which is directed the deepest aspiration of the human spirit as expressed in its quest for God and also in its quest, through its tending toward God, for the full dimension of its humanity, or in other words for the full meaning of human life" (*Redemptor Hominis,* No. 11). By appropriating in this way the best of the religious thought of others into their own life of faith, men and women of dialogue experience certain aspects of the sublime convergence of all creatures in the One who is their Creator and fulfiller.

It is the deep desire of believers for unity that impels them to do all that they can to eliminate prejudice and suspicion, enabling people to see in each other that which they really are and that which they want to be. This same desire takes them beyond the egoism and the chauvinism of self-centered groups and helps them to prevail over theological exclusivism. In the commonly held monotheistic faith of Muslims, Jews and Christians they see convincing proof that the unifying will of God will have the last word. In the face of the accusation too often made that religions have been causes of division and wars, believers, holding Abraham as their model, must give proof of the contrary by translating their faith in the One, Living and Subsistent God into deeds of human solidarity and friendship. The diversity of their particular approaches to the mystery of God's oneness does not in any sense detract from the commonality of their monotheistic faith. Rather, it gives an incentive for each tradition to clarify its unique expressions of thought for the sake of others. Let the different religious communities emulate each other, then, in sharing their spiritual experiences, and thus respond better to the challenges of the modern world and to the questioning of contemporary women and men.

This quest for unity that motivates both Christians and Muslims in their religious dialogue is somewhat similar to the ecumenical movement[1] that tries to bring together all those who profess Jesus Christ as their only Savior. Pope John Paul II has called attention to the qualities of those who engage in ecumenical work, that is, loyalty, perseverance, tenacity, humility and courage. In that statement he concluded, "What we have just said

must also be applied—although in another way and with the due difference—to activity for coming closer together with the representatives of
the non-Christian religions, an activity expressed through dialogue, con-
tacts, prayer in common, investigation of the treasures of human spirituality, in which, as we know well, the members of these religions also are not
lacking" (*Redemptor Hominis,* No. 6).

The following suggestions are based on possible elements of convergence at the level of the common life led by Christians and Muslims in
which both personally and as communities they give expression to their
feelings and convictions. The divine mystery, the gift of God's Word, the
role of prophets, the existence of communities, the secrets of prayer and
the ways of holiness are so many "stations" of the mystical journey of
those believers who meet and share with one another in their desire to
obey God alone and to conform to His reconciling purpose.

I
THE DIVINE MYSTERY

Christians and Muslims find common ground with the Jews in con-
templating the unsearchable mystery of the hidden God who transcends
all things. The Psalmist cried, "Who is God, but the Lord? And who is a
rock, except our God?" (Psalm 18:31). Truly, "the Lord is God; there is
no other besides Him" (Deuteronomy 4:35), and "we know no other god
but him" (Judith 8:20). He is "the Alpha and the Omega" (Revelation
1:8), the one who does not change (Malachi 3:6). "He does not faint or
grow weary" (Isaiah 40:28) because He is "the everlasting God" (Isaiah
40:28), the living Lord (Jeremiah 4:2), the one who is "alive forevermore"
(Revelation 1:18).

Muslims in turn exalt this transcendence by linking it closely with the
mysterious unity of "the Living One Who dieth not" (Qur'an 25:58). "He
is Allah, the One! Allah, the eternally Besought of all!" (Qur'an 112:1, 2).
"Allah's are the fairest names" (Qur'an 7:180), and "with Him are the
keys of the Invisible" (Qur'an 6:59). The so-called "Throne Verse" affirms, "There is no God save Him, the Alive, the Eternal. Neither slumber
nor sleep overtaketh Him. Unto Him belongeth whatsoever is in the
heavens and whatsoever is in the earth. Who is he that intercedeth with
Him save by His leave? He knoweth that which is in front of them and
that which is behind them, while they encompass nothing of His knowledge save what He will" (Qur'an 2:255).

Christians also realize that their words are mere babbling, as they,
along with their Jewish and Muslim brethren, stand in awe before the

mystery of God, and say, with Saint Paul, "Oh the depth of the riches and wisdom and knowledge of God! How unsearchable are His judgments and how inscrutable His ways! For who has known the mind of the Lord, or who has been His counselor?" (Romans 11:33–34). But thanks to the teaching of Jesus they know that "in the beginning was the Word, and the Word was with God, and the Word was God" (John 1:1), and that "the Word became flesh" (John 1:14), so that "to all who received Him . . . He gave power to become children of God" (John 1:12). This is why they can only thank God, saying with Saint Paul, "Blessed be the God and Father of our Lord Jesus Christ, who has blessed us in Christ with every spiritual blessing. . . . He destined us in love to be His sons through Jesus Christ" (Ephesians 1:3–5).

Although the two faiths have different approaches to the mystery of divine transcendence, they can nevertheless find common ground in discussing the ways in which theology and mysticism use language to talk about the ineffable greatness of that mystery. Christians are not strangers to the supreme sense of transcendence expressed by Muslims. Before the time of Islam and in continuity with the Jews, Christians struggled against idols, rejected the cult of emperors and opposed every form of human deification. What is more, the revelation of the Christian mysteries can only be understood through the threefold affirmation of a transcendence that upholds the complete freedom of God.

Is it right to put the Almighty God confessed by Muslims in opposition to the God of love confessed by Christians? Is it appropriate always to say that Muslims believe in a God who is the Supreme Being, the Creator of all things, the Sovereign Law-giver for humankind and the Righteous Judge of all human deeds, whereas Christians find in God a Father of infinite love, a Word entering the world of humankind to lead them to Him, and a Spirit upholding the divine unity while acting to bring all human beings together? On the one hand it is obvious that although Christians and Muslims worship the same God, the ways they represent Him are not at all the same. But, on the other hand, when Muslims say constantly that God is mercy and pardon, when they designate Him by the special name, "The Merciful One (*Al-Rahman*)," are they so different from Christians who say, with Saint John, "God is love, and he who abides in love abides in God, and God abides in him" (I John 4:16)?

Christians and Muslims have many thoughts and questions to share with each other regarding their experience of faith. We have seen that in both communities believers should emulate the Beautiful Names of God so that, in some measure, their lives become a certain representation of the divine attributes. With such an aim in view they should clarify to each other how they understand and interpret the Beautiful Names of God in their respective traditions. Here the saints and mystics, with their particular gifts, have something to say, since their testimony about God expands and transforms the scriptural and theological elements in which it is rooted.

II
THE GIFT OF THE WORD

Both Christians and Muslims believe that God took the initiative in history to speak to human beings, thus revealing to them many truths about the mystery of His being and about the hidden destiny of humankind. Believers in both religions consider themselves the fortunate beneficiaries of the "gift of the Word." To Muslims the Qur'an is the final, unique and fully authentic manifestation of the Word of God, addressed to humankind through the ministry of Muhammad. "And thus have We inspired in thee (Muhammad) a Spirit of Our command" (Qur'an 42:52). And, from their side, Christians are persuaded that "in many and various ways God spoke of old to our fathers by the prophets; but in these last days He has spoken to us by a Son, whom He appointed the heir of all things" (Hebrews 1:1–2). In fact, "no one knows the Son except the Father, and no one knows the Father except the Son and any one to whom the Son chooses to reveal Him" (Matthew 11:27). It would be fitting, then, that both parties spend much time clarifying to each other the ways in which their respective religions receive and understand the Word of God. Islam recognizes a privileged status for Jews and Christians by calling them "People of Scripture," and anyone can see that the Qur'an is preeminently the holy book of Muslims.

In this connection we should point out the different ways in which the two religions identify the Word addressed to them by God. For Muslims this Word is the Qur'an itself, ". . . a revelation of the Lord of the Worlds . . . in plain Arabic speech" (Qur'an 26:192, 195), and mention has already been made of its importance for them as discourse about God and as a law for humankind. According to the Christian view, the Word of God came into the world "in the fullness of time," not in the form of a Scripture, but in the person of Jesus Christ, revelation of the Father and presence of God in the world of human beings. For Christians "sacred tradition and sacred Scripture form one sacred deposit of the Word of God, which is committed to the Church" (*Dei Verbum*, No. 10), for "there exist a close connection and communication between sacred tradition and sacred Scripture . . . both of them flowing from the same divine wellspring" (*Dei Verbum*, No. 9).[2] Consequently, the holy books of the

Old and New Testaments, jointly the work of God and the divinely inspired authors, are only one means, albeit an exceptional and normative means, of coming to know the Word of God in life's experience.

For a dialogue to be authentic the partners must take account of this profound difference so as to avoid useless confusion and irrelevant criticism. In the Muslims' religious experience, the Word of God "became perfect Scripture," namely the Qur'an, whereas Christians believe that the Word of God "became flesh," as a perfect man in the person of Jesus Christ.

Those in dialogue have much to say to each other about the significance of this gift of the Word in their religious experience. What are their normal, though diverse, approaches to the mystery of the "God who speaks," and what are the attitudes cultivated in their meditation of the Word and their submission to its precepts? What they have in common is a respect for the Word of God and a desire to meditate upon it in order better to conform to it in life. Both religions enjoy rich resources of commentary and exegesis that can contribute to a fuller understanding of their complementary points of view in dealing with both the Qur'an and the Bible. In this regard a "spirituality of openness" should help Muslims and Christians alike to share their insights on the human acceptance of the Word in their respective traditions.

The Word of God constitutes an ever-actual message of power filled with ever-fresh richness of meaning for believers. Muslims and Christians can experience together the living quality of the Word as they consider their various methods of reading and meditating it, the ways in which that Word is applied to the growth of the human spirit and the challenge of its meanings to present-day realities. In a wholesome spirit of mutual emulation they will find that the Word accomplishes its purpose only when it is respoken as a human word, as a fresh affirmation by believers of their commitment to God in love and service to others.

III
THE ROLE OF PROPHETS

Christians and Muslims recognize that the sending of prophets is a "mercy from God" in behalf of human beings. Both have as a part of their tradition the ideal of the "prophetic model," because they believe that God chooses for Himself certain messengers, purified and sanctified by Him, to be His preferred servants and faithful transmitters of His Word. Previously we noted how, for Muslims, the succession of prophets culminated in the mission of the "Seal of the Prophets," Muhammad, the venerated Prophet of Islam. In the Christian view, the person of the Word Incarnate is "more than a prophet," since Jesus came to fulfill the hope of the prophets and the expectation of Israel.

While recognizing this fundamental difference regarding the fulfillment or the transcending of prophecy, as well as the criteria for ideal prophecy, Muslims and Christians, along with Jews, are alike stressing the importance of the mission of prophets in the religious history of humanity. People need spiritual guides who are both like them and unlike them, and who speak to them of righteousness and love, who show them truths about God and about themselves, and who, although contradicted and persecuted, demonstrate an example of patient faithfulness while awaiting the final victory of God Himself.

More than anything the prophet is a witness (*shahid*) who finally, after carrying out his mission in spite of dangers and trials, stands humbly aside before the person of the One who sent him. The prophet is, like John the precursor, "the voice of one crying in the wilderness: Prepare the way of the Lord" (Mark 1:3). Is not the most important task "to raise up children to Abraham" (Matthew 3:9) who "do what Abraham did" (John 8:39)? The call of the prophets still rings in the ears of believers today, appealing to them also to be courageous witnesses for God, so that humanity might hear even now the message of the Lord, with its demands and its promises.

IV
THE SUPPORT OF COMMUNITIES

Both Muslims and Christians are aware that they are never alone in living their faith. The former belong to a vast community (*umma*) which constitutes "the abode of justice and peace" on earth, intended by God for the choice ones of His creatures, those who have willingly submitted to Him by confessing their "islam." The latter likewise belong to a Church whose catholicity makes it able to embrace all ages, all peoples and all cultures. It is both visible institution and mystical body, the place where Jesus Christ continues mysteriously to be present and active among people. All believers need a vital fellowship in which to nourish their faith, develop their life of worship, express their hope and exercise their love and concern for others.

Realistically, however, there is a great difference between the expectation of many Muslims that history will see the development of Islamic civilization in the earth and the theological view of Christians who see the "People of God" gathered in the Church but scattered among diverse political, economic and cultural systems. The present situations of political and cultural pluralism seem to indicate that we should make some distinction between religious communities that meet as believers and political groupings that bring people together as citizens.

On the level of their communities of faith Christians and Muslims experience similar problems and dangers. Both suffer from internal dissension caused by diversity of ceremonial practices, opposition of schools of thought and disagreement of leaders. It should be useful to share with each other the experience of efforts exerted to protect the unity of the community in the midst of diversity.

Another danger lies in the attitude of those holding exclusivist theologies, who would condemn other believers notwithstanding the sincerity of their heart, the purity of their conscience and the reality of their religious experience. Can we not dare to accept one another, not as adversaries or as rivals, but as "sisters and brothers in God," called to practice Abrahamic hospitality toward all those who seek the face of God? This would imply that we respect the religious community of the others, its places of worship and its legitimate representatives, that we recognize the other community as a place where its members can be nurtured in faith, and that we gratefully acknowledge any evidences of holy living that we observe among them. In so doing, Christians and Muslims will show their willingness to go beyond the narrow limits of their particular communities and to think seriously together about the validity of the many "religious families" that exist, situating their discussions in the light of the inscrutable decrees of the God who saves. Such efforts are even more needed in view of the fact that Christians and Muslims often have to take a stand together against the theological challenge of non-monotheistic religions as well as respond together to the aspirations and quest of their own coreligionists who most readily reach out beyond their own community.

V
THE SECRETS OF PRAYER

Christians and Muslims are called to be praying people, for prayer is an essential part of the worship that they owe to the one, living and true God. Consisting of postures and words of varying significance, prayer expresses both the submission of the body and the readiness of the soul. In Islam as well as in Christianity ritual prayer, prescribed by the regulations of worship, and spontaneous prayer, depending on individual initiative, have both developed many methods and styles. Nevertheless, for the two

religions prayer has the same deep meaning, worship of God and identification with His will, in spite of the differences that they have in their
approaches to the divine mystery. Christians cannot but respect and admire the faithful Muslims whom they observe performing the ritual
prayer (*salat*) five times a day. And when Muslims attend the Liturgy of
the Hours or the Eucharistic Prayer of the Christians, they feel interest
and sympathy. Both groups would do well to deepen their knowledge of
the various forms of prayer in the other community. A dialogue of believers can facilitate the mutual discovery of the riches of prayer that each
group has accumulated through the centuries. Is not prayer, as a Muslim
author says,[3] the "banquet of the monotheists"?

Muslims and Christians organize their lives around the practice of
regular prayer whereby, through invocation and thanksgiving, they integrate their time, their work, their joys and their sorrows into the exercise
of sincere worship. By means of the daily cycle of prayers and festivals
Christians and Muslims make the events of their lives, all of the important
stages of human experience, from birth until death, the focus for prayer
and thanksgiving. Thus, it would be a source of enrichment for any person to find out more about how those from the other faith "sanctify life"
through the structure of prayer.

The spiritual experience of Christians and Muslims, both personal
and communal, is very rich and sometimes takes on unexpected forms.
Both communities practice praise and thanksgiving, offer prayers of request and supplication, and prayers for forgiveness. For the formulation
of these prayers they make use of the rich store of sacred texts in their
respective traditions. The many forms of prayer help believers to understand better what should be their proper attitude in worship, as they seek
to fulfill the calling which they believe that they have received from the
Lord. Muslims know that their simple and yet demanding worship
(*'ibada*) must be the act of a humble servant (*'abd*). Filled with reverent
awe (*taqwa*) and submissive devotion (*khushu'*), they confess in prayer
their total commitment, their submissiveness and their abiding gratitude.
They declare their love for the Law, their desire to be forgiven by the One
who is "Hearer, Knower" (Qur'an 58:1), and their longing to be finally
brought near to their Lord, "content in His good pleasure" (Qur'an
89:28). Christians have learned from Jesus Christ how they should pray to
"His Father and their Father" (John 20:17) as beloved children "predes-
tined to be conformed to the image of His Son" (Romans 8:29). It is as
such that they confess to Him their filial love, their willing obedience and
their complete dedication. In prayer they come to know how great is the
love that transforms them, how grave the sin that disfigures them and how
completely Jesus Christ has become reconciliation for all, so that He

might dwell in their hearts through faith (Ephesians 3:17) and "be the first-born among many brethren" (Romans 8:29), to the end that all might enter into "the fullness of God" (Ephesians 3:19). Remarkable indeed are both the similarities and the differences between Muslims and Christians in their life of prayer and worship. These two related ways of devotion show how extremely varied are the gifts of God to His servants and provide exceptional opportunities for dialogue.

Sometimes Muslims and Christians feel the need to pray together, and they realize immediately how difficult it is to do so. The best course seems to be for each group to respect entirely the ritual prayer and official acts of worship of the other faith, without ever trying to participate directly in them, but maintaining a readiness to be present as sympathetic observers at those times of worship whenever invited, in the name of Abrahamic hospitality. Especially to be avoided are insistent invitations to those of the other religion and too easy assumptions of similarity between the two ways of worship. Some people would interpret these as forms of disguised proselytization and others would take them as a syncretistic tendency. The same thing might be said regarding the holy books and the official texts which provide the unique expression of the faith of each group. Primarily the Qur'an belongs to Muslims and the Fatiha is their particular prayer, even as the New Testament belongs first of all to Christians, and the Lord's Prayer is the unique expression of their faith. We show our respect for the faith of others when we avoid any suggestion of incorporating them into our way or of trying to take them over. On the other hand we can hope that from both sides the example of mystics and saints will provide the necessary incentive for the creation of common forms of praise and supplication that can bring them together in an experience of shared prayer.

VI
THE WAYS OF HOLINESS[4]

In both religious traditions mystics and saints have always been considered as exceptional witnesses and models, although to different degrees. Christians continue to hear Jesus Christ say to them, "Unless your righteousness exceeds that of the scribes and Pharisees, you will never enter the Kingdom of heaven" (Matthew 5:20), for "you ... must be perfect, as your heavenly Father is perfect" (Matthew 5:48). The Apostles, such as Peter, John and Paul, were the first to respond to this call. That is why Peter could write, "As He who called you is holy, be holy yourselves in all your conduct; since it is written, 'You shall be holy, for I am holy' "

(I Peter 1:15–16). In his turn John wrote, "Let us love one another; for love is of God, and he who loves is born of God and knows God" (I John 4:7). For his part Paul added, "God is faithful, by whom you were called into the fellowship of His Son, Jesus Christ our Lord" (I Corinthians 1:9).

Muslims have always been attracted by the example of early believers in their spiritual tradition, who tried to live according to the Qur'an in every respect and who observed scrupulously the model of behavior given by the Prophet Muhammad. A hadith on the subject of the love of God (*mahabba*) says that "when God loves one of His servants, He tries him; if that servant is steadfast, God sets him apart. If he shows contentment with his lot, God chooses him. . . . And when God loves him with great love, God takes possession of him by taking everything away from him." This is why many Muslims have felt constrained to investigate the "secret merits" (*asrar*) of their principal rites and to go deeply into the various levels of faith. Without going into the controversies that surround the development of mysticism (*tasawwuf*) in Islam and the way in which some have sought to extend its practices to the masses of believers within the framework of religious brotherhoods (*turuq*), it must be recognized that many great mystics have given their witness through the centuries and that certain of their sayings have universal relevance.

Christians and Muslims, then, would benefit greatly if they took the time to learn together about the marvelous experiences attempted, lived and described by these exceptional men and women. Their history is one of failure and of grace, of egoism and of self-giving, of mediocrity and of holiness. Every effort of self-purification on the way toward God requires the same disciplines, such as examination of conscience, control of desires, restraint of the tongue, detachment from the world, surrender of all earthly possessions, renunciation of all forms of prestige, abandonment of all pride and ambition. The first steps in a mystical approach to God are marked by the renewing grace of conversion, the strength coming from confidence in God, thanksgiving, godly fear and hope, poverty and detachment. Finally, through meditation upon the oneness of God and surrender to his providence, the way leads to a state of ardent desire, loving familiarity and tranquil nearness.

Thus, the spiritual adventure of mystics and saints, with its characteristic symbolic language and solutions proposed to specific problems, should make possible a fundamental dialogue between Christians and Muslims. The experience of these "seekers after God" has always developed most fully along with a sense of divine transcendence. When Muslims give witness to their faith in the One God they are well aware that God alone can rightfully say of Himself, "There is no God save Him" (Qur'an 39:6). Human beings can only give their lips, their hearts and their spirits in order to become a very humble earthly echo of the divine voice. And when Christians pray, saying, "Abba, Father," they are well aware that only the eternal Word is capable of saying "Father" to the One who manifests Himself eternally through that Word in the unity of the Spirit. Human beings can only repeat that ineffable name "through Jesus Christ, by Jesus Christ and in Jesus Christ," who is the perfect Son. At the end of this discussion of their profound spiritual experiences, Muslims and Christians find themselves at last confronted with the mystery of death. How can death be endured and vanquished in the sure hope that God will reveal to all "that which he has prepared for his chosen ones, things unseen by any eye, unheard by any ear, and unimagined by the human mind."[5] This is "beyond dialogue" and belongs to God alone.

Notes

1. The expression, "ecumenism of the People of Scripture," is somewhat ambiguous. Out of respect for Jewish and Muslim partners in dialogue, Christians should not apply too quickly a term ("ecumenism") to their activity that has been reserved, up to now, uniquely to describe specific efforts to attain unity in Jesus Christ. In addition, according to the Qur'an and the Islamic tradition, the title, "People of Scripture," is reserved for Jews and Christians only, so Muslims could justly say that the expression does not include them.

2. Here the whole document of the Second Vatican Council, *Dei Verbum,* regarding "Divine Revelation," should be studied.

3. Ibrahim al-Bajuri, an Egyptian Muslim theologian (1783–1860), author of many textbooks that reflect the teaching of Sunni Islam at Al-Azhar in Cairo.

4. See the papers read during a colloquium on "Holiness in Islam and Christianity," held at the Pontifical Institute of Arabic and Islamic Studies, Rome, and published in *Islamochristiana,* No. 11 (1985): Ziaul Hasan Faruqi, "The Concept of Holiness in Islam," pp. 7–27; John Carroll Futrell, "The Concept of Christian Holiness," pp. 29–36; Suzanne Le Gal, "Models of Holiness for Christians," pp. 37–50; K.A. Nizami, "Models of Holiness for Muslims," pp. 51–67; Jean-Marie Gaudeul, "A Christian Critique of Islamic Holiness," pp. 69–90; Mahmoud Ayoub, "A Muslim Appreciation of Christian Holiness," pp. 91–98.

5. This is a famous "divine hadith" (*qudsi*) that will remind Christians of the words addressed by Saint Paul to the Corinthians of his time (I Corinthians 2:9), using, as he did, a text from Isaiah 64:3 and expanding its meaning enormously.

Conclusion

Christian-Muslim dialogue should be seen as one of the principal dimensions of life for men and women of faith in those many countries where believers in the two religions live, work, love, suffer and die together. No doubt many Christians in such circumstances choose to be indifferent, leaving the two communities to their respective customs, prejudices and integrity. However history has shown that such an attitude keeps each party involved in ignorance of the other and encourages all the more misunderstanding, suspicion and conflict. Some Christians today show a particular interest in the historical aspects of Islam, but at the risk of misunderstanding its religious dimensions, those features that make it possible for those who belong to Islam to experience God and to give witness of their faith. The dialogue proposed is meant to take place on the level of the human spiritual adventure, and, in this book, the point of view is specifically Christian. We all realize, of course, that Islam, for its part, has a double aim, in that it is both a plan for the everyday life of society and a plan for human religious experience. By taking the first plan into account we have tried to assess here the likelihood and the limits of dialogue today in terms of the second plan, that is, a "religious dialogue" between Christians and Muslims.

Having begun in the Middle East and around the Mediterranean basin this dialogue has spread to all continents. This fact increases its chances for success since Christians and Muslims find themselves in a great variety of national and ideological situations, in ever-changing political and economic contexts. They are never alone, just the two of them, and they often find themselves confronted, sometimes in the company of their Jewish friends, by the impressive religious development of non-monotheistic believers, as is the case in Asia. In addition the world of technology and the evolution of modernity challenge Muslims and Christians to renew the expressions of their faith and to rethink the terms of their dialogue. Taking account as it does of all human and religious factors, the dialogue enjoys almost unlimited possibilities as to place, time, manner and procedure. So, believers in the two religions can hope to develop a true exchange that will be marked by acceptance of one another, mutual understanding of the two faiths, sharing of experiences and taking initiatives under the guidance of the Spirit. Requiring first of all the acceptance by its partners of the divine requirements for such a discipline, the way of dialogue leads quite naturally into the mystery of the human personality and its free response to the call of the Lord. Dialogue can never be simply an end in itself, for it remains at the disposal of God to serve the cause of fuller conciliation between believers.

Such an enterprise requires that each person recognize the values of the other. This means that Christians and Muslims must overcome the ignorance of the past, forget the injustices of other times, and renew their knowledge and appreciation of one another. Only after such a renewal of knowledge about and esteem for Muslims can Christians undertake a theological evaluation of Islam in the light of the Gospel, regarding it as a monotheistic and prophetic religion having ties—not yet well defined— with the Judeo-Christian tradition, and as a faith in which the Abrahamic model of faith and submission to God is upheld in all of its implications.

At the same time Christians and Muslims must face realistically, in faith, the obstacles that stand in their way: a history of fourteen centuries during which polemics and conflicts have often prevailed over mutual understanding and cooperation, so that the attitudes of the communities confronting each other are marked by instinctive distrust and prejudice. The only way to eliminate such attitudes is to persevere in imparting accurate information and practicing greater love for one another. From their side, Christians will repudiate the often unjustified accusations that ignorant people make so easily against Islam. And they will seek to know better exactly what Muslims think about Christians, their Scriptures, their mysteries, their monotheism, their Church and their efforts to be faithful to the message of Jesus. We need to be aware that there are limits to dialogue so that we might avoid setbacks in relationships with one an-other. But it is especially in projects of common action that Christians and Muslims will give evidence of their reconciliation, as they cooperate in programs based on values held in common with one another and equally, more or less, with other people of good will. In all situations human collaboration is necessary.

Then, beyond this action together, dialogue between Christians and Muslims must consider seriously what religious convergence is possible. It would be a pity if the encounter and sharing of the two parties should be limited in scope to the temporal values of this world. Higher values are involved in the spiritual quests of believers, and when they take these into account they discover that they have much to share with each other on the level of their respective religious experiences. By participating in this shar-ing the faith of the partners is purified and deepened. Christians and Muslims find themselves oriented toward a kind of spiritual emulation which can only draw them closer to each other. As they articulate their parallel and distinct ways of faithfulness to the religious traditions from which they draw their life, there is nothing to prevent them from entering into a common hope, that of seeing God enlighten them concerning whatever spiritual convergence is possible for them, in expectation of the time when finally he will inform them of that wherein they differ (Qur'an 5:48).

As they make their way together Christians and Muslims should develop their dialogue on the four levels necessary for human communication. First there is the generous sharing as brothers and sisters, which is a dialogue of hearts. Next is the dialogue of life, requiring the courage to expend themselves in the promotion of human values, of which God alone is the final guarantee. In the dialogue of speech the partners dare to make discourse on both God and humankind. And finally there is the resolute dialogue of silence in which God speaks directly to the heart of each of the partners. Truly it is in silence that real dialogue begins and ends, since it is in the silence of faith that each one can catch a glimpse of the eternal destiny of the other.

Christians, from their side, feel called by Jesus Christ to extend in the present time His work as mediator, the one who reconciles those who are far away with those who are near. As their Master, they know that they must take the first steps and accept in their prayer and in their heart "whatever is true, whatever is honorable, whatever is just, whatever is pure, whatever is lovely, whatever is gracious, [whatever] is [of] any excellence, [whatever] is . . . worthy of praise" (Philippians 4:8). In their personal dialogue with the Father, in the name of Jesus Christ, they have the privilege of experiencing already, in the Spirit, this reconciliation of all people in the One who is the object of their expectancy, praise and devotion. They realize that the dialogue is not always easy, and that sometimes they will be contradicted or misunderstood, even rebuffed or rejected. Dialogue is then an extended "passion" through which Christians have a part in the Cross and Resurrection of the One who has already "broken down the dividing wall of hostility" (Ephesians 2:14), and who has given to them "the ministry of reconciliation" (II Corinthians 5:18).

Appendix

Many official and unofficial meetings have taken place between variously qualified representatives from the Christian and Muslim communities over the past fifteen years, especially since the time when the Second Vatican Council began to encourage such meetings. In addition to gatherings of Orientalists, Arabists, and other specialists, where Christians and Muslims consider only the economic, cultural and political aspects of their relationship, there are more and more meetings being held where the partners, Christians and Muslims, decide to base their conversations on their religious experience and place them in the framework of their respective religious communities. Some of these meetings were held at the initiative of individual persons or private groups, whereas others were set up by official organizations of the Catholic Church and of the World Council of Churches, as well as by corresponding groups in the Islamic world.

The Secretariat for (Relations with) Non-Christians was established by Paul VI in the season of Pentecost 1964 (May 19), and it has been headed in turn by Cardinal Marella (1964–73), Cardinal Pignedoli (1973–80), Archbishop Jadot (1980–84) and Cardinal Arinze. This office has a small permanent staff in Rome and a membership composed of Bishops of local Churches.[2] It calls upon a number of consultants in various countries for help in its work. On October 22, 1974 a Commission for Islam was formed, composed of a group of specialists as consultants. This Commission was added to the already existing Office for Islam. The staff at the Secretariat participate in the activities organized by local Churches and sometimes take initiatives themselves when needed, whether it be to set up a dialogue with Muslims, with people of the great Asian religions (Hinduism and Buddhism) or with those from the African traditional religions. Since May 1966 the Secretariat has published a *Bulletin* in two languages, and has also produced a number of other publications whose main titles are listed in the Bibliography. In its regular meetings the Secretariat seeks to bring Bishops of the Churches together with consultants in order to follow the development of dialogue throughout the world. It works in collaboration with other Congregations and Secretariats of the Holy See and with the World Council of Churches.

As a result of various preparatory meetings and the Declaration of Intent of Addis Ababa (January, 1971), the Commission on World Mission and Evangelism of the World Council of Churches decided to create a Sub-Unit for Dialogue with People of Living Faiths and Ideologies (DFI), with its headquarters in Geneva. This Sub-Unit has a Section for Islam and a Section for Judaism. The Section for Islam has been responsible for a number of activities in Africa and in Asia, thanks to the dynamic efforts of its secretary. Recently, in Chiang Mai, Thailand, the Sub-Unit sponsored an important Theological Consultation on Dialogue in Community (April 18–27, 1977), at which an attempt was made to give the first comprehensive report of efforts at dialogue by the WCC. This Sub-Unit publishes reports and papers in the *International Review of Mission* (Geneva). It works in close collaboration with the Secretariat for Non-Christians in Rome.

Below are listed, in chronological order, the most important recently organized occasions for dialogue between Christians and Muslims.

1969 (March 2–6): Geneva-Cartigny (Switzerland), upon the initiative of the WCC Commission on Faith and Order. About twenty Christians and Muslims discussed the following themes: (1) The Word of God and Holy Scripture; (2) Religion in a world dominated by technology; (3) The outlook for Muslim-Christian dialogue.

1970 (December 16–29): Rome, on the initiative of the Secretariat for Non-Christians. A delegation from the High Council of Islamic Affairs in Cairo met with representatives from the Roman Secretariats of the Holy See.

1972 (July 12–18): Broumana, Lebanon, on the initiative of the DFI (WCC). A group of twenty-five Christians and twenty Muslims discussed "In Search of Understanding and Cooperation." The final *Memorandum* emphasized as the "guiding principles of dialogue": frank witness, mutual respect and religious freedom.

1974 (July 17–21): Accra, Ghana, on the initiative of the DFI (WCC). Eleven Christians and nine African Muslims discussed the theme: "The Oneness of God and the Human Community: Cooperation between African Muslims and Christians in Work and Witness."

1974 (September 10–15): Cordoba, Spain, on the initiative of the Spanish Association for Muslim-Christian Friendship. About a hundred Christian and Muslim participants from Arab countries and Europe discussed the following four themes: "The Christian View of Islam"; "The Muslim View of Christianity"; "Reciprocal Implications of Political and Religious Expansion"; "The Crisis of Faith and Experiences in Religious Education."

1974 (September 9–16): Cairo, Egypt. At the invitation of the High Council for Islamic Affairs in Cairo, a delegation from the Secretariat for Non-Christians met with Egyptian representatives of Islam.

1974 (October 24–27): Rome. At the invitation of the Secretariat for Non-Christians, a delegation from Saudi Arabia, headed by the Minister of Justice, met with representatives from the Holy See to discuss human rights as seen by the two religious traditions.

1974 (November, 11–17): Tunis, Hammamet and Kairouan, Tunisia, on the initiative of the Center for Economic and Social Studies and Research (CERES) of the University of Tunis. Twenty-eight Muslims and thirteen Christians, all experts in their field, discussed: "European Muslim and Christian Responses to Problems of Development." They also heard reports on present-day trends in biblical and Quranic studies.

1975 (January 4–10): Hong Kong, on the initiative of the DFI (WCC). About thirty Muslims and Christians discussed "Muslims and Christians in Society: Mutual Consultation and Cooperation in Southeast Asia."

1976 (February 1–6): Tripoli, Libya, on the initiative of the Arab Socialist Union and in cooperation with the Secretariat for Non-Christian Religions. About three hundred and fifty Muslims and one hundred and fifty Christians from fifty-five countries of Asia, Africa and Europe heard papers and discussed: "Religion and Ideology"; "Doctrinal Common Ground in the Two Religions and Places for Meeting in Various Areas of Life"; "Faith and Social Justice"; "How to Overcome the Prejudices and Misunderstandings that Divide Us."

1976 (June 26–30): Geneva-Chambésy, Switzerland, on the initiative of the DFI (WCC). A group of nine Christians and four Muslims discussed the difficult problems of "Christian Mission and Muslim Da'wa."

1977 (March 21–27): Cordoba, Spain, on the initiative of the Spanish Association for Muslim-Christian Friendship. About two hundred Christians and Muslims from Arab countries and Europe heard papers and discussions on "Muhammad and Jesus As Prophets."

1977 (November 14–18): Beirut, Lebanon. On the initiative of the DFI (WCC), about twenty Muslims and Christians discussed, "Faith, Science and Technology and the Future of Humankind," dealing with the ecological, socio-political and theological aspects of the subject.

1978 (April 12–13): Cairo, on the initiative of the Egyptians. A delegation from the Secretariat for Non-Christians was received by the religious authorities at Al-Azhar University to exchange views on "Possibilities for Dialogue Between Christians and Muslims."

1979 (March 12–13): Geneva-Chambésy, Switzerland. On the initiative of the DFI (WCC), a group of five Muslims and ten Christians studied developments in dialogue and made plans for future meetings. The theme was "Christians and Muslims Living Together."

1979 (April 30–May 4): Tunis, Tunisia, on the initiative of the CERES of the University of Tunis. About sixty Muslim and Christian scholars from Arab countries, Europe and America discussed "The Meanings and Levels of Revelation" within the two religious traditions.

1980 (November 3–6): Beirut, Lebanon. On the initiative of the WCC (Middle East Office) and of the Lebanese Cenacle, about thirty Christian and Muslim experts (twenty of whom were Lebanese) analyzed "The Most Recent Developments in Muslim-Christian Dialogue" as well as new opportunities for future activities.

1982 (March 30–April 1): Colombo, Sri Lanka. On the initiative of the DFI (WCC) and with the official participation of the Karachi World Islamic Council, a group of Christians and Muslims, all of whom were members of programs of aid for development and charitable organizations, discussed the need for collaboration both in their aims and methods, with the hope of forming a joint committee to study the possibilities for cooperation.

1982 (May 24–29): Tunis, Tunisia. On the initiative of the CERES of the University of Tunis, about sixty Muslim and Christian scholars exchanged views on "The Participation of Muslims and Christians in the Cause of Human Rights."

1985 (May 6–7): Rome. On the initiative of the Secretariat for Non-Christians and with the collaboration of Vidyajyoti Institute of Delhi (India), eleven Muslim and Christian scholars, coming from India, Pakistan and Bangladesh, exchanged views on "Holiness in Islam and Christianity" at the Pontifical Institute of Arabic and Islamic Studies with other scholars resident in Rome.

1985 (August 19): Casablanca, Morocco. At the invitation of King Hasan II, Pope John Paul II delivered an address to an audience of eighty thousand young Muslims at the stadium: "Our common fellowship as believers in God and our commitment to build a new world in accordance with God's plan."

1986 (March 3–7): Porto-Novo, Benin. On the initiative of the DFI (WCC), thirty African Christians and Muslims discussed the theme: "Relations between religions and the state, education and family, in Africa."

1986 (April 21–26): Tunis, Tunisia, on the initiative of the CERES of the University of Tunis, about fifty Muslim and Christian scholars, coming mainly from Arab countries and France, exchanged views on "Spirituality: a necessity of our times."

1987 (September 27–October 2): Kolymbari, Crete (Greece). At the invitation of the DFI (WCC), twenty Muslim and Christian scholars coming from the Middle East and Western Europe discussed "the place of religious pluralism in today's structures and the role of believers in promoting mutual trust and community."

1984–1988 (Windsor-Amman). On the initiative of the Royal Academy of Jordan for Islamic Civilization Research (Al Albait Foundation) and of St. George's House (Windsor Castle), four Muslim-Christian Consultations have been organized bringing together between thirty and forty Anglicans and other Christians and Jordanian Muslims, alternately in Windsor (November 15–18, 1984): "Muslims, Christians and Jews: towards increasing dialogue in the promotion of common values," in Amman (October 28–30, 1985): "Common concerns and values for family life," in Windsor (May 29–31, 1987): "Ethics and business," and in Amman (September 17–18, 1988): "Ethics and banking."

1986–1988 (Geneva-Chambésy and Amman). On the initiative of the same Academy and of the Foundation of the Orthodox Centre of the Ecumenical Patriarchate of Geneva-Chambésy, three Muslim-Christian Consultations were held by about forty or fifty Orthodox and other Christians and Jordanian Muslims alternately in Geneva-Chambésy (November 17–19, 1986): "Authority in the state, in society and in the family," in Amman (November 21–23, 1987): "Muslim and Christian co-existence in history and today; common values: work, freedom and environment," and in Geneva-Chambésy (December 12–15, 1988): "Peace and justice: Bible and Qur'an, Human rights and Jerusalem."

To the above should be added meetings for Muslim-Christian dialogue on a national level, such as in India, France or elsewhere, wherever secretariats have been established by Conferences of Bishops[3] or by Councils of Churches. Also there have been many unofficial initiatives by local, national and international groups desiring to engage in theological study regarding dialogue[4] or to promote friendly human relations between believers.[5]

A few preliminary conclusions may be drawn from these many efforts at meeting and discussion. Organized dialogue is still in its beginning stages, so it cannot be expected to have achieved all of the results desired. Experience has proven, however, that it is in practicing dialogue that we learn to dialogue, provided, of course, that each party retains its integrity while trying to understand the other fully. A Moroccan Muslim professor said, "Dialogue presupposes partners who are different. Other persons are only 'other' because they are not 'I.' Let us have no apologetics, no proselytism. To make concessions ourselves or to require others to make them would be to betray the spirit of dialogue."

Opportunities at present for dialogue may be summarized as follows:

1. The political and culture climate makes it possible for Muslims and Christians to meet in a spirit of full equality.

2. Attitudes are changing.

3. The challenges of the modern world are extremely serious and urgent.

4. The need for joint humanitarian effort is more and more pressing.

On the other hand the following difficulties are apparent:

1. Dialogue has sometimes been too official and formal.

2. Discussions have sometimes to pass through stages of polemics or deliberate conciliation before they become true dialogue.

3. Dialogue almost always has political overtones.

4. People who want to dialogue have great difficulty in making impartial judgments, in listening carefully to others and in going beyond their own view of things.

5. Too often participants have tried to deal with many subjects at the same time and have too easily given in to improvisation and vagueness.

Some people would like to see large conferences on simple and concrete themes (such as, "Needful Areas of Human Cooperation") which would sensitize Christian and Muslim public opinion. Then the study of more difficult questions (such as "Possible Areas of Religious Convergence") would be reserved for small, permanently constituted groups in which mutual friendship and esteem would have time to grow and would contribute to more positive long-term results. In either case prayer, silence and meditation are very important to the end that all might hear God and thus learn to listen better to their partners in dialogue. Thus the "brotherhood in God" will open the way to the "brotherhood of humankind."

Notes

1. For the whole history of organized occasions for dialogue, see Maurice Borrmans, "The Muslim-Christian Dialogue of the last ten years," in *Pro Mundi Vita* (Brussels), No. 74, Sept.–Oct. 1978, 58pp. (large format), with bibliography; *Meeting in Faith: Twenty Years of Christian-Muslim Conversations Sponsored by the World Council of Churches,* compiled by Stuart E. Brown, WCC, Geneva, 1989, ix-181pp.; *Faith in the Midst of Faiths (Reflections on Dialogue in Community),* ed. S.J. Samartha, WCC, Geneva, 1977, 200pp.

For a detailed report of each of the meetings noted here see the different issues of the journal *Islamochristiana* (IPEA, Rome).

2. On June 28, 1988, Pope John Paul II signed and promulgated the Apostolic Constitution *Pastor Bonus,* which restructured and renamed many curial offices. The Secretariat for

Non-Christians was renamed the Pontifical Council for Interreligious Dialogue. These changes took effect on March 1, 1989.

3. Such as the Secretariat for the Church's Relations with Islam in France, cf. Michel Lelong, "Le Secrétariat de l'Eglise de France pour les Relations avec l'Islam," in *Islamochristiana*, No. 4 (1978), pp. 165–174.

4. Such as "The Muslim-Christian Research Group" in North Africa and Europe: cf. Robert Caspar, "Le Groupe de Recherches Islamo-Chrétien," in *Islamochristiana*, No. 4 (1978), pp. 175–186; each subsequent issue of *Islamochristiana* carries a report of the GRIC's activities.

5. Such as l'Association de la Fraternité Religieuse (al-Ikha' al-Dini) in Egypt: cf. in *Islamochristiana*, No. 5 (1979), pp. 253–258.

Bibliography

I
ISLAM

A. General Survey

Denny, Frederick Mathewson. *An Introduction to Islam.* New York: Macmillan, 1985.
Eaton, Charles Le Gai. *Islam and the Destiny of Man.* Albany, NY: State University of New York (SUNY) Press, 1985.
Esposito, John. *Islam: the Straight Path.* New York & Oxford: Oxford University Press, 1988.
Gibb, H.A.R. *Islam,* 2nd Edition. New York & Oxford: Oxford University Press, 1975.
Guillaume, Alfred. *Islam.* London: Penguin, 1961.
Nasr, Seyyed Hossein. *Ideals and Realities of Islam.* Winchester, Mass.: Unwin Hyman, 1983.
Watt, W. Montgomery. *What is Islam?* London: Longmans Green, 1968.

B. For a Deeper Study

Anderson, J.N.D. *Islamic Law in the Modern World.* New York: New York University Press, 1959.
Azzam, Abd al Rahman. *The Eternal Message of Muhammad.* New York: Mentor Books, 1965.
Coulson, N.J. *A History of Islamic Law.* Edinburgh: The University Press, 1964.
Cragg, Kenneth. *Counsels in Contemporary Islam.* Edinburgh: The University Press, 1965.
Cragg, Kenneth and Speight, R. Marston. *The House of Islam,* 3rd Ed. Belmont, CA: Wadsworth, 1988.
———. *Islam from Within: Anthology of a Religion.* Belmont, CA: Wadsworth, 1980.
Gibb, H.A.R. *Modern Trends in Islam.* Chicago: University of Chicago Press, 1947.
Hodgson, Marshall G.S. *The Venture of Islam* (3 vols.) Chicago: University of Chicago Press, 1974.

Rahman, Fazlur. *Islam and Modernity: Transformation of an Intellectual Tradi-
tion.* Chicago: University of Chicago Press, 1982.
Smith, Wilfred Cantwell. *Islam in Modern History.* Princeton: Princeton Univer-
sity Press, 1957.
Tabataba'i, Muhammad Husayn. *Shi'ite Islam.* Edited and translated by Seyyed
Hossein Nasr. Albany, NY: State University of New York Press, 1975.

C. Tools for Scholarly Research

Brockelmann, Carl. *History of the Islamic Peoples.* New York: Capricorn Books,
1960.
The Cambridge History of Islam, 2 Vols. Cambridge: Cambridge University
Press, 1970.
Al-Faruqi, Isma'il R. and Al-Faruqi, Lois Lamya'. *The Cultural Atlas of Islam.*
New York: Macmillan, 1986.
Hitti, Philip Khuri. *History of the Arabs from the Earliest Times to the Present,*
10th Ed. New York: St. Martin's Press, 1970.
Hollister, John Norman. *The Shi'a of India.* London: Luzac, 1953.
Jeffery, Arthur. *A Reader on Islam.* Hague: Mouton, 1962.
Shorter Encyclopedia of Islam. London: Luzac & Co., Leiden: Brill, 1961.
Trimingham, J. Spencer. *Islam in East Africa.* Oxford: Oxford University Press,
1964.
———. *Islam in the Sudan.* London: Cass, 1965.
———. *Islam in West Africa.* Oxford: Oxford University Press, 1959.

II
THE QUR'AN

A. Translations

Ali, A. Yusuf. *The Holy Qur'an.* Lahore: M. Ashraf, 1934.
Arberry, Arthur J. *The Koran Interpreted.* Oxford: Oxford University Press, 1964.
Irving, T.B., Tr. *The Qur'an: The First American Version.* Brattleboro, VT:
Amana Books, 1985.
Pickthall, Mohammed Marmaduke. *The Meaning of the Glorious Koran.* New
York: Mentor Books, n.d.

B. Studies

Ayoub, Mahmoud. *The Qur'an and Its Interpreters,* Vol. I. Albany, NY: State
University of New York (SUNY) Press, 1984.

Cragg, Kenneth. *The Event of the Qur'an.* London: Allen and Unwin, 1971.
———. *The Mind of the Qur'an.* London: George Allen & Unwin, 1972.
Jeffery, Arthur. *The Qur'an as Scripture.* New York: R.F. Moore Co., 1952.
Rahman, Fazlur. *Major Themes of the Qur'an.* Minneapolis & Chicago: Bibliotheca Islamica, 1980.
Von Denffer, Ahmed. *'Ulum al-Qur'an: An Introduction to the Sciences of the Qur'an.* Leicester, England: The Islamic Foundation, 1983/1403 A.H.
Watt, W. Montgomery. *Bell's Introduction to the Qur'an.* Edinburgh: University Press, 1970.

III
MUHAMMAD

Cragg, Kenneth. *Muhammad and the Christian: A Question of Response.* Maryknoll, NY: Orbis Books, 1984.
Haykal, Muhammad Husayn. *The Life of Muhammad.* Translated by Isma'il Ragi A. al-Faruqi. Indianapolis: North American Trust Publications, 1976.
Lings, Martin. *Muhammad: His Life Based on the Earliest Sources.* Rochester, VT: Inner Traditions International, Ltd., 1983.
Schimmel, Annemarie. *And Muhammad is His Prophet: The Veneration of the Prophet in Islamic Piety.* Chapel Hill and London: The University of North Carolina Press, 1985.
Watt, W. Montgomery. *Muhammad at Mecca.* London: Oxford University Press, 1953.
———. *Muhammad at Medina.* London: Oxford University Press, 1956.
———. *Muhammad, Prophet and Statesman.* London: Oxford University Press, 1961.

IV
ISLAMIC THEOLOGY AND MYSTICISM

Abduh, Muhammad. *The Theology of Unity.* Translated by Ishaq Musa'ad and Kenneth Cragg. London: Allen and Unwin, 1966.
Arberry, Arthur J. *Sufism.* London: George Allen and Unwin, 1950.
von Grunebaum, Gustave E., Ed. *Theology and Law in Islam.* Wiesbaden: Harrassowitz, 1971.
Nasr, Seyyed Hossein, Ed. *Islamic Spirituality: Foundations.* New York: Crossroad, 1987.
Nicholson, Reynold A. *The Mystics of Islam.* London: Routledge and Kegan Paul, 1966.
Padwick, Constance E. *Muslim Devotions.* London: S.P.C.K., 1961.

Schimmel, Annemarie. *The Mystical Dimensions of Islam.* Chapel Hill: University of North Carolina Press, 1975.

Trimingham, J. Spencer. *The Sufi Orders in Islam.* London: Oxford University Press, 1973.

Watt, W. Montgomery. *The Formative Period of Islamic Thought.* Edinburgh: The University Press, 1973.

———. *Islamic Philosophy and Theology.* Edinburgh: University Press, 1962.

Wensinck, A.J. *The Muslim Creed: Its Genesis and Historical Development.* London: Frank Cass & Co., 1965.

V
ISLAM AND POLITICS

Enayat, Hamid. *Modern Islamic Political Thought.* Austin: University of Texas Press, 1983.

Esposito, John L., Ed. *Islam and Development: Religion and Sociopolitical Change.* Syracuse: Syracuse University Press, 1980.

———. *Islam and Politics.* Syracuse: Syracuse University Press, 1984.

Levy, R. *The Social Structure of Islam.* Cambridge: University Press, 1965.

Watt, W. Montgomery. *Islamic Political Thought.* Edinburgh: University Press, 1968.

VI
ISLAM AND CHRISTIANITY

Borrmans, Maurice. "The Muslim-Christian Dialogue of the last ten years." *Pro Mundi Vita,* 74 (Sept.–Oct. 1978).

British Council of Churches. *Relations with people of other faiths: Guidelines on Dialogue in Britain.* London: B.C.C., 1981.

Brown, David. *A New Threshold.* London: B.C.C., 1976.

Camps, A. *Partners in Dialogue: Christianity and other World Religions.* New York: Orbis Books, 1983.

Caspar, R., et al. *Trying to Answer Questions,* Rome: Pontifical Institute of Arabic and Islamic Studies, 1989.

Chukwulozie, V. *Muslim-Christian Dialogue in Nigeria.* Ibadan: Daystar Press, 1986.

Cracknell, Kenneth. *Towards a New Relationship: Christians and People of Other Faith.* London: Epworth Press, 1986.

Cragg, Kenneth. *Alive to God: Muslim and Christian Prayer.* Oxford: University Press, 1970.

———. *Jesus and the Muslim: An Exploration.* London: George Allen and Unwin, 1985.

———. *The Call of the Minaret,* 2nd Edition. Maryknoll, NY: Orbis Books, 1985.
Daniel, Norman A. *The Arabs and Mediaeval Europe.* London: Longmans, 1975.
———. *Islam and the West.* Edinburgh: University Press, 1960.
Gaudeul, J.M. *Encounters and Clashes: Islam and Christianity in History,* Vol. I Survey, Vol. II Texts. Rome: Pontifical Institute of Arabic and Islamic Studies, 1984.
———. "Learning from Polemics." *Encounter,* 75 (May 1981).
Haines, Byron L. and Cooley, Frank L., Editors. *Christians and Muslims Together: An Exploration by Presbyterians.* Philadelphia: Geneva Press, 1987.
Kritzeck, J. *Peter the Venerable and Islam.* Princeton: University Press, 1964.
Parrinder, Geoffrey. *Jesus in the Qur'an.* London: Sheldon, 1965.
Rousseau, R.W., Ed. *Christianity and Islam: the Struggling Dialogue.* Scranton: Ridge Row Press, 1985.
Southern, R.W. *Western Views of Islam in the Middle Ages.* Cambridge: Harvard University Press, 1978.
Speight, R. Marston. *Christian Muslim Relations: An Introduction for Christians in the United States of America.* Hartford: Office on Christian-Muslim Relations of the NCC, 1983.
———. *God is One: The Way of Islam.* New York: Friendship Press, 1989.
Tritton, A.S. *The Caliphs and their non-Muslim Subjects.* London: Cass, 1970.
Tudtud, Bienvenido S. *Dialogue of Life and Faith. Selected Writings of Bishop Bienvenido S. Tudtud.* Quezon City, Philippines: Claretian Press, 1988.
Vatican II Council. *Declaration on Non-Christian Religions,* (Nostra Aetate).
Watt, W. Montgomery. "The Christianity criticized in the Qur'an." *Muslim World,* (1967), pp. 197–201.
———. *Islam and Christianity Today.* London: Routledge-Kegan Paul, 1983.
Wingate, A. *Encounter in the Spirit: Muslim-Christian Meetings in Birmingham.* Geneva: WCC, 1988.
World Council of Churches. *Meeting in Faith: Twenty Years of Christian-Muslim Conversations Sponsored by the World Council of Churches.* Compiled by Stuart E. Brown. Geneva: WCC, 1989.
———. *Christian Presence and Witness in Relation to Muslim Neighbours.* Geneva: WCC, 1981.
———. *Guidelines for Dialogue.* Geneva: W.C.C., 1979.
———. *My Neighbour's Faith and Mine: Theological Discoveries through Interfaith Dialogue. A Study Guide.* Geneva: WCC, n.d.
———. *Current Dialogue.* Periodical.
Young, W.G. *Patriarch, Shah and Caliph.* Rawalpindi, Pakistan: Christian Study Centre, 1974.

Useful bibliographies and articles can be found in the pages of these two periodicals published by the Pontifical Institute of Arabic and Islamic Studies of Rome (Viale di Trastevere, 89, 00153 Rome):

——— *Encounter,* monthly
——— *Islamochristiana,* annual

VII
PUBLICATIONS OF EPISCOPAL CONFERENCES AND OF THE VATICAN SECRETARIAT FOR NON-CHRISTIAN RELIGIONS

Abbott, W. *The Documents of Vatican II.* London and Dublin: G. Chapman. See in particular: "The Church" (Lumen Gentium), pp. 14–102; "Revelation" (Dei Verbum), pp. 111–129; "Missions" (Ad Gentes), pp. 584–631; "Religious Freedom" (Dignitatis Humanae), pp. 675–697; "Non-Christians" (Nostra Aetate), pp. 660–669.

"Asian Bishops meet at Kuala-Lumpur, Nov. 1979." *Encounter,* 66 (June 1980).

"Christians in North Africa: The meaning of our encounters with Muslims (Pastoral Letter of Bishops of North Africa)." *Encounter,* 73–74 (March 1981).

Publications of the Pontifical Council for Inter-Religious Dialogue (00120 Vatican City):

"The Hope which is in us." Brief presentation of the Catholic faith to Non-Christians, Vatican Press, 1967.

"Towards the meeting of Religions." Suggestions for Dialogue, Vatican Press, 1967.

"Religions—Fundamental themes for dialogistic understanding." Rome: Ancora, 1970.

"Chiesa e Islam: Addresses of Pope John Paul II on Islam." Vatican City: Secretariat for non-Christians, 1981. In Arabic, English and French.

"The Attitude of the Church towards the Followers of Other Religions." Vatican Press, 1984.

Bulletin. Bilingual periodical, published three times a year.

Index

Abortion, 72–73, 94
Abraham, 52, 93, 109; covenant
with, 35; hospitality of, 31, 100,
107, 109; and monotheism, 15;
as prophetic model, 50–51, 66,
101, 106; submission to God,
45, 47, 50–51, 65
Abu Bakr, 20
Abu Ra'ita al-Takriti, 14
Adam, 45, 90
Adultery, 73
Africa, 18, 21
Agha Khan, 21
Ahmadis, 21
Al-Aqsa mosque, 20
Al-Ghazali, 60, 64, 98
Al-Mawdudi, 21
Al-Safi Ibn al-Assal, 14
'Ali, 20–21
'Allal al-Fasi, 72
Almsgiving, 61–62, 65
Apostolate, duty of, 85–86
Arab League, 19–20
Arab Summit meetings, 20
Arinze, Cardinal, 115
Arts and culture, development of,
95
Asceticism, 64
Ash'arism, 71
Asin y Palacios, Miguel, 15
Ataturk, Kemal, 19
Atheism, 92

Baha'is, 21
Bangladesh, 17

Barnabas, Gospel of, 78–79
Beatitudes, 23, 83, 92–93
Birth control, 73

Charity, 61–62
China, 18
Christian-Muslim dialogue:
acceptance of one another, 31–
32, 41–42; adapting to each
other, 33; contradictory aspects
of, 41; conversion to God, 38–
39; cooperation, areas of, 88–99;
dynamic aspects of, 33–34;
elimination of prejudice, 70–77;
false effort at accommodation,
38; human imitation of divine
action, 97–99; in Middle Ages,
13–14; mutual understanding,
32–33; in name of God, 37–38;
participants, 13–27; past
wrongs, 68–70; and proselytism,
42–43, 85; reconciliation with
one another, 38–39; religious
agreement, areas of, 100–11;
religious dimensions of, 36–43;
and religious minorities, 86;
spiritual emulation, 39–40; *see
also* specific headings, e.g.;
Family; God
Christianity, Muslim view of, 77–
84; church as only earthly
power, 81–82; falsification of
Christian scriptures, 77–79; as
limited polytheism, 80–81;
rejection of Christian mysteries,

128

79–80; unfaithfulness to Jesus' message, 82–83
Christians: churches and communities, 15–17; and faith of others, 34–36; *see also* Christian-Muslim dialogue
Community: "Community of the Prophet," 58–59, 74; and confession of faith, 60; conscience of, 58–59; leadership, 21; "maternal community," 17, 58; "People of the Community," 59; solidarity of community of believers, 58–59; support of communities, 106–07; unanimous counsel of, 20
Conference of Islamic Countries, 20
Creation, 88–89
Cultural development, 95

Declaration on the Relation of the Church to Non-Christian Religions, 15, 26, 51, 65, 66, See also *Nostra Aetate.*
Dietary restrictions, 84
Dignity. *See* Human dignity
Divorce, 73
Druses, 21

Ebner, Ferdinand, 1
Economic justice, 95–96
Elias of Nisibis, 14
Ethics, 72–73

Faith, 37–38, 60, 65, 75–76; confession of faith, 60, 64; without works, 62
Family: and Christian-Muslim dialogue, 29; dignity of, 94–95; moral standards, 22–23; *see also* Marriage

Fanaticism, 73–75
Fasting, 61, 65
Fatalism, 71
Fatiha, 109
Fatimids, 21
Fear, Islam as religion of, 76–77
"Festival of sacrifice," 51
Fornication, 73
Francis, Saint, 14

God, 16; Beautiful Names of, 60, 61, 76, 103–04; dialogue "in name of God," 37–38; Divine Mystery, 102–04; love of, 16, 76; mercy and pardon, 76, 99, 103; submission to, 16, 45–47, 50–51, 65, 76; transcendence, 16, 59–61, 76, 80, 102–04; Word of God, 104–05
Gospel, 78

Hadith, 59, 64
Hanafites, 20
Hanbalites, 20
Hasan al-Banna, 21
Holiness, 109–11
Holy war, 74–75
Homosexuality, 73
Human dignity, 23; and atheism, 92; of the conscience, 91; of freedom, 91–92; of life, 91; of marriage and the family, 94; and organization of society, 93–97; origin, 90; promotion of, 91–92; of the spirit, 91
Human rights, 16, 24, 93
Humanitarian service, 89–93
Hunayn Ibn Ashaq, 14

Ibn Taymiyya, 80
Imams, 20–21
Incarnation, 41, 80